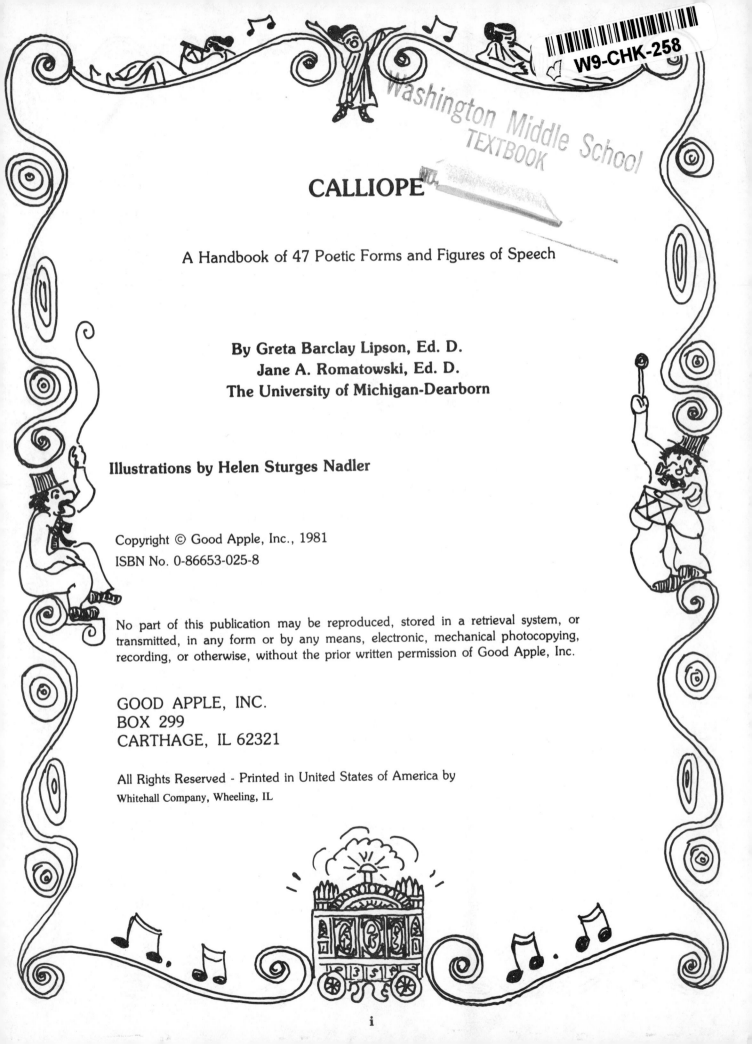

CALLIOPE

A Handbook of 47 Poetic Forms and Figures of Speech

By Greta Barclay Lipson, Ed. D.
Jane A. Romatowski, Ed. D.
The University of Michigan-Dearborn

Illustrations by Helen Sturges Nadler

Copyright © Good Apple, Inc., 1981
ISBN No. 0-86653-025-8

GOOD APPLE, INC.
BOX 299
CARTHAGE, IL 62321

All Rights Reserved - Printed in United States of America by
Whitehall Company, Wheeling, IL

We dedicate this book
To all the hard working teachers
Who share our vision --
Searching for a way
To make language work for children.

TABLE OF CONTENTS

Introduction

WHY POETRY WRITING?

Why poetry writing? Why any art form? Poetry writing like other art forms provides a viable option for self-expression. Through creative writing people define the world around them, conceptualize it and capture its ambience. Through creative writing people can define their relationship to the world, to others in it, and perhaps, most importantly, they can define themselves.

Poetry writing in the classroom is important for the nurturing of creative thinking, for imagery, for fantasy, and for self-expression. How else can writing talent be found and nurtured? How else can young children discover themselves to be competent, sensitive writers? The goal of poetry writing in any classroom is the opening up of the world of poetry to children *beyond* the elements of rhyme alone and exploring the poetic and lyric qualities of prose and nonrhyming forms.

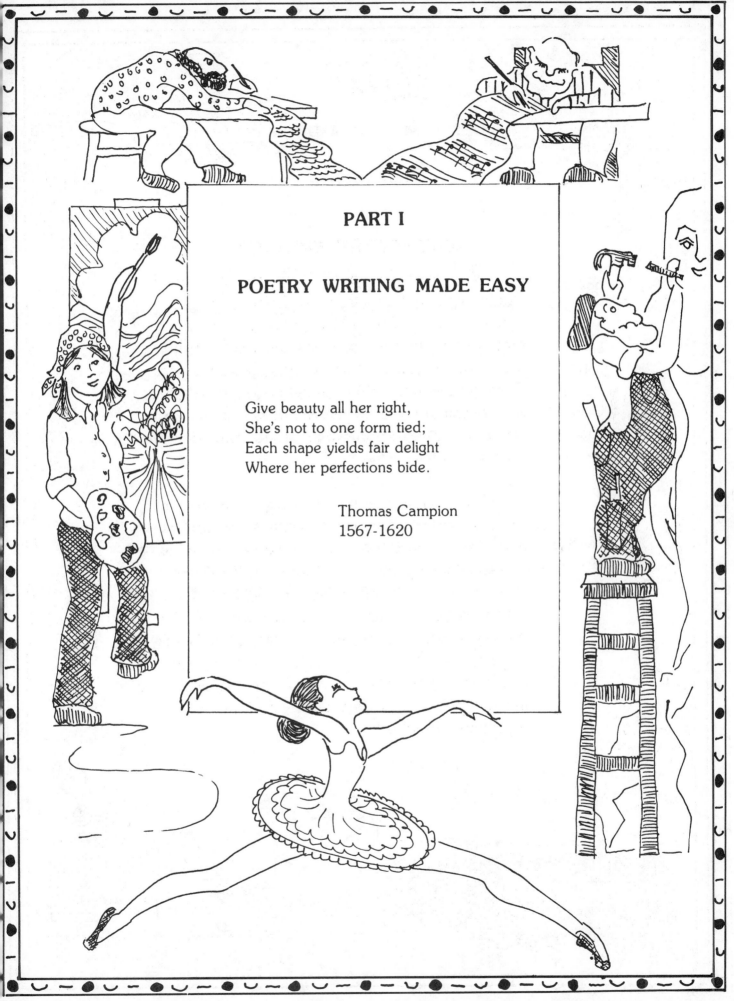

PART I

POETRY WRITING MADE EASY

Give beauty all her right,
She's not to one form tied;
Each shape yields fair delight
Where her perfections bide.

Thomas Campion
1567-1620

Part I

POETRY WRITING MADE EASY

Here is a simple guide that will help you take your students through poetic forms with which they can work effectively. We see it as a nice, neat package for learning and pleasure. The plan is eclectic. We have drawn from many sources. There will be forms you recognize and others newly encountered. You will find differences in definition and construction as you know them, because we too encountered these variations in our research. But be adventuresome, since many patterns have been simplified over the years for working with children. Some poetic forms will give you pause and you may say, "That's not poetry!" -- to which we respond, "Try it. The lyric product may be well worth the effort."

We must remember that poetry, according to *Webster's Dictionary,* is "writing that formulates a concentrated imaginative awareness of experience in language chosen and arranged to create a specific emotional response through meaning, sound and rhythm. A quality that stirs the imagination."

In light of the human experience with language, we can also say that poetry is:

An expression of power and sensitivity in written form.

A guide for children through the wondrous possibilities of their own language.

A reflection of the world of yesterday and today.

A lyric and personal expression.

An experience with the color, flavor and magnificence of words.

A compression of thought and feeling.

An adventure with figurative speech.

A constellation of forms from serious and dramatic to lighthearted and nonsensical.

An expression in rhyme, free verse or prose.

An experiment with language.

A challenging lesson in vocabulary, word choice and grammar.

A distilled language response to life, to an event, to a moment.

A disciplined expression of thought and feeling in language.

An introduction to a range of self-selected topics of wide appeal to boys and girls.

A song intended to be read aloud, heard, savored and enjoyed.

Freedom to exercise poetic license and take liberties not allowed in ordinary writing.

As modern as the stuff of today and as old as the hills.

GUIDELINES FOR TEACHING

THE MATERIALS IN THIS BOOK

1. Wherever possible, read *many* examples of the poetry you wish your students to experience writing. Feature such poems on the chalkboard daily, or make bulletin board displays of them.

2. Take time to enjoy the poetry. Highlight the interesting language. Ask students to select words or phrases which they consider powerful.

3. When some saturation has occurred, engage students in a whole-class activity that will result in the poetic form desired. You, the teacher, will be the scribe. Students will be the idea-generators.

4. Discuss the elements, the rhyming pattern, the physical arrangement, etc.

5. Be sensitive to the amounts of practice needed. Some groups can be released to a poetic form after one or two whole-class practices. Others need much more practice over an extended period of days before they are comfortable enough to launch on their own.

6. Encourage partnerships for those who are reluctant to try on their own.

7. Be sure to end an experience in writing with an experience in reading. At this time, listen respectfully, acknowledge contributions, and repeat words and phrases that are exceptional.

INITIAL POETRY

★ Many things in our environment can serve as a springboard for writing poetry. For example, using the initials of one's name provides a base from which the class can build some exciting free verse. Three initials are necessary. If a teacher or student has only two, then a middle initial is selected to represent a name one would like. If a person has more than three initials, then one is simply deleted. This idea, initial poetry, works well when teachers volunteer their initials first and list them at the top of three columns on the chalkboard, thus:

J   A   R

With the aid of the students, a brainstorming session is conducted for brief, picturesque phrases which begin with the letters posted. Highlight the qualities desired by contributing phrases yourself. In a while your board will begin looking like this, perhaps:

J	A	R
Joyful Jane	Across the deep blue lake	Resolving problems well
Jangling keys	Approaches life calmly	Renew my spirit
Junipers swaying softly	Angers those around	Roping steers
	Acrobats dangling dangerously	Running wildly
		Racing across town

Now, on fresh chalkboard space, select a phrase from the "J" column that appears to have some good follow-up phrases in columns "A" and "R." Write that phrase on the board as the first line of your free verse, for example:

> Junipers swaying softly

Now read it to the class -- "poetically." Ask students to read through the "A" column to find a phrase that would follow well. When a decision is made, write it as the second line.

> Junipers swaying softly
> Across the deep blue lake

Now repeat the process for the third line. Write it down, and read the finished poem to the class.

> Junipers swaying softly
> Across the deep blue lake
> Renew my spirit

Try other combinations with the entire class. Erase. Use some other student's initials, use the initials of a famous person, a movie star, a cartoon hero, or even the three letters on the license plate of the family car (provided your state uses three letters).

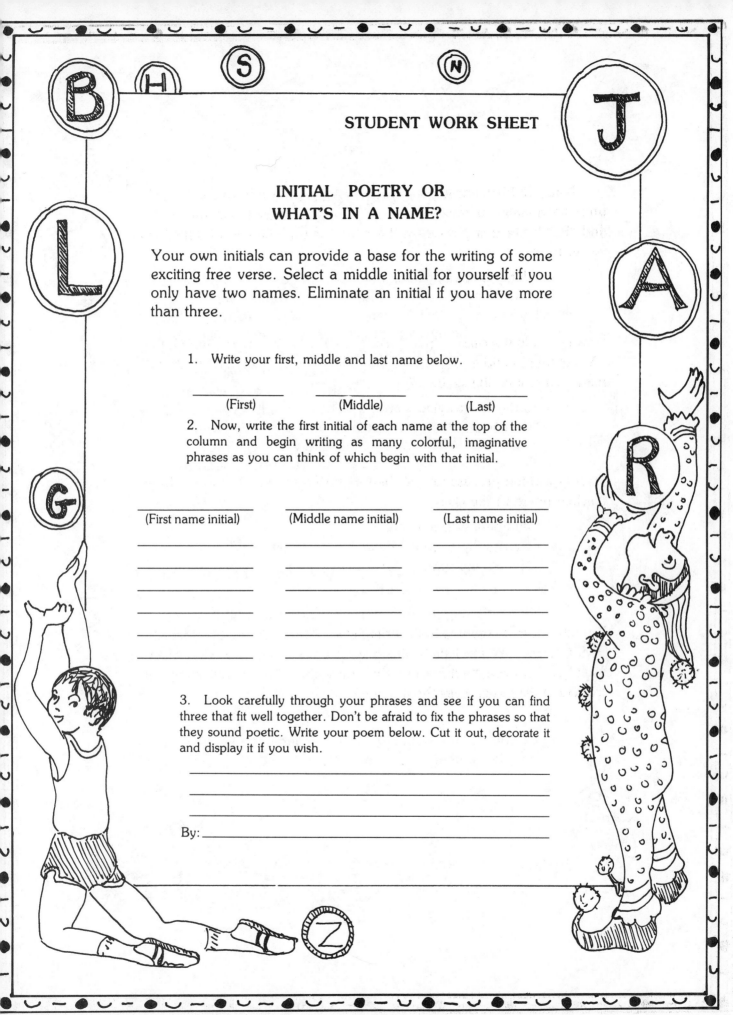

STUDENT WORK SHEET

INITIAL POETRY OR
WHAT'S IN A NAME?

Your own initials can provide a base for the writing of some exciting free verse. Select a middle initial for yourself if you only have two names. Eliminate an initial if you have more than three.

1. Write your first, middle and last name below.

    _____   _____   _____
    (First)   (Middle)   (Last)

2. Now, write the first initial of each name at the top of the column and begin writing as many colorful, imaginative phrases as you can think of which begin with that initial.

_____   _____   _____
(First name initial)   (Middle name initial) (Last name initial)
_____   _____   _____
_____   _____   _____
_____   _____   _____
_____   _____   _____
_____   _____   _____

3. Look carefully through your phrases and see if you can find three that fit well together. Don't be afraid to fix the phrases so that they sound poetic. Write your poem below. Cut it out, decorate it and display it if you wish.

_____

_____

_____

By: _____

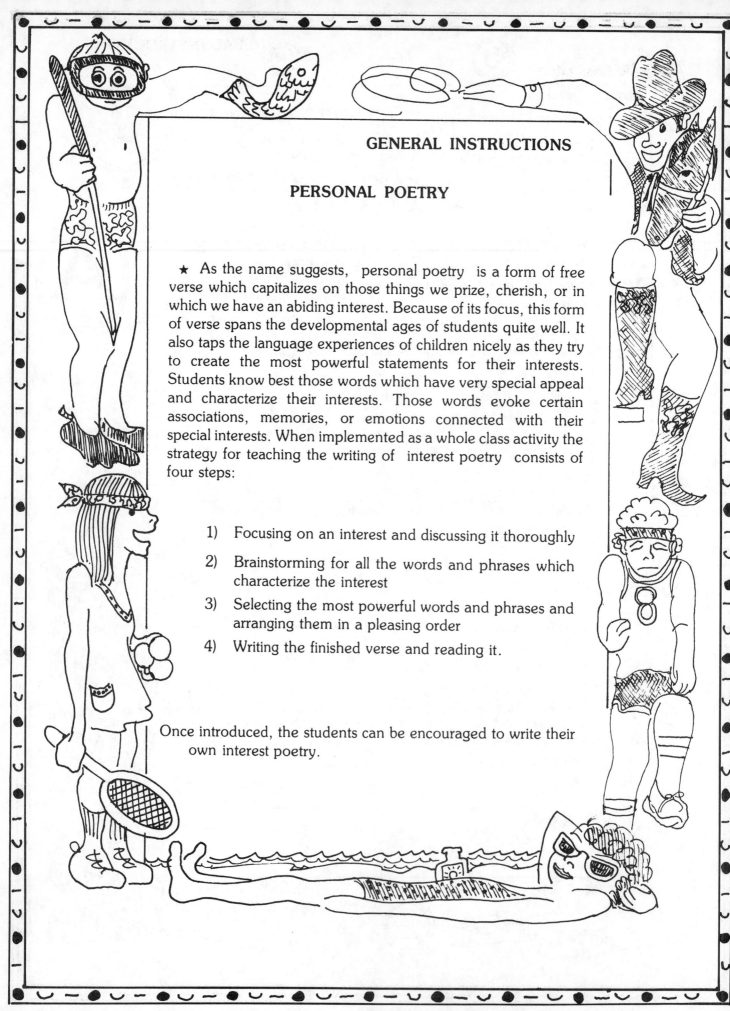

GENERAL INSTRUCTIONS

PERSONAL POETRY

★ As the name suggests, personal poetry is a form of free verse which capitalizes on those things we prize, cherish, or in which we have an abiding interest. Because of its focus, this form of verse spans the developmental ages of students quite well. It also taps the language experiences of children nicely as they try to create the most powerful statements for their interests. Students know best those words which have very special appeal and characterize their interests. Those words evoke certain associations, memories, or emotions connected with their special interests. When implemented as a whole class activity the strategy for teaching the writing of interest poetry consists of four steps:

1) Focusing on an interest and discussing it thoroughly

2) Brainstorming for all the words and phrases which characterize the interest

3) Selecting the most powerful words and phrases and arranging them in a pleasing order

4) Writing the finished verse and reading it.

Once introduced, the students can be encouraged to write their own interest poetry.

Sample class effort:

1. Focus: Baseball

2. Ideas generated in brainstorming:

power hitters	slugger's row
all-American sport	souvenirs
strike	hot dogs, peanuts, popcorn
grand slam	the umpire's blind
diamond	kill the umpire
triple play	rabid, loyal fans
you're out	sunburned bleacherites
the old ball game	America's passion
hoarse shouting - wild cheers	hometown heroes
foul ball	*Doubleday's diamond

   *(Abner Doubleday invented baseball in 1830, in Cooperstown, New York.)

3. Final interest poem
   Baseball
   The old ball game
   All-American sport
   Sunburned bleacherites
   Hot dogs, peanuts, popcorn
   Hoarse shouting -- wild cheers
   Strike, foul ball, "Kill the umpire!"
   Hometown heroes -- slugger's row
   Grand slam!
   Doubleday's diamond
   America's passion.

Here is another interest poem with a different focus:

   Sunbathing
   Welcome! I missed you for so many months
   Come warm my spirit, sun
   Creep into my flesh
   Me -- greasy with lotion
   Half awake -- half asleep
   Thoughts simmer in the heat
   Freckles coming to a slow boil
   Burn me sun. Burn me.

PERSONAL POETRY
SPOTLIGHTING AN INTEREST -- WITH POETRY

Personal poetry is a form of free verse which emphasizes personal interests! Here is an opportunity to write a poem which will highlight a keen interest of yours.

1. Name an interest of yours. _____

2. Now write as many words and phrases which come to your mind about your interest.

_____   _____   _____

_____   _____   _____

_____   _____   _____

_____   _____   _____

_____   _____   _____

3. Use the work space below to "play around" with the words and phrases. Think carefully about what would sound best first, in the middle, and at the end. Remember the first line is the word you wrote in step #1. Make your poem as short or as long as you wish.

_____

_____

_____

_____

_____

_____

4. When you are satisfied with your poem, write it in your best writing on the back of this sheet and illustrate it.

CLERIHEW: BIOGRAPHIC POETRY

★ The clerihew is a form of rhymed poetry named after its creator, Edmund Clerihew Bentley. It is light verse based upon a person's name. It should tell something about the individual and is often humorous. It consists of four lines (a quatrain) which uses the rhyming pattern a a, b b. The first line consists of the person's name. To facilitate rhyming, think carefully about which name (first or last) should be at the end of the first line -- which would be capable of generating more rhyming words.

1.   Jane Kisselbaum

or   2.   Kisselbaum, Jane

As a class activity select a name -- a famous person or a fictitious name is good for starters. Write the name on the board in both versions as we did above, and allow the class to discuss which name lends itself best to rhyming. Then, generate as many rhyming words as possible for the end word. In our example, the second choice is more amenable to rhyming, and a possible list of rhyming words for "Jane" might be:

rain	slain	wane
sane	mane	vane
gain	dane	bane
feign	cane	plain
deign	pane	etc.
vain	reign	

Using the generated list of rhyming words, guide students into creating a second line. When a selection is **arrived** at, write the couplet (a two-liner) on the board. Perhaps it would read,

Kisselbaum, Jane
Was extremely vain

Now, have students generate some possible third lines. Again brainstorm for all the possible rhyming words to the end word in the third line. Then construct your fourth line and complete your clerihew. It could read:

Kisselbaum, Jane (a)
Was extremely vain, (a)
Her life she'll pass (b)
Before a looking glass! (b)
        J. Romatowski

Another example:
Alexander Bevy (a)
Was terribly heavy (a)
He felt like a whale (b)
When he stood on the scale! (b)
        G. Lipson

A word of caution — some students find rhyming to be very difficult. Whole class practices as suggested here will not only facilitate the writing of a clerihew which is the immediate goal, but will also arm the students with a strategy they can use in any writing requiring rhyme. This activity is a good one for partnership writing and for work with a thesaurus. The most important feeling for students to experience is one of competence in writing rhyme. Your "sixth sense" should be activated on this occasion so that no student leaves the experience feeling inadequate.

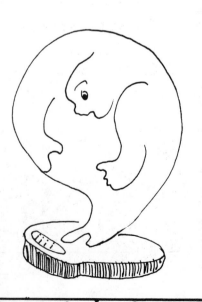

CLERIHEW - BIOGRAPHIC POETRY

Clerihew is a form of biographic light verse based upon a person's name. It should tell something about the individual and is often humorous.

1. Pick a name from the telephone book which interests you. Write it here.

_____

2. Decide which name is best for the end word of your first line. Write the name here.

_____

3. Think of as many rhyming words as you can for the end word of your first line.

_____   _____   _____
_____   _____   _____
_____   _____   _____
_____   _____   _____
_____   _____   _____

4. Now create a second line for your poem using one of the rhyming words. Write it on the line below.

_____

5. Think of a good third line for your poem. *Keep the sense* of your two first lines going. Write your third line below.

_____

6. Think of as many rhyming words as you can for the end word of your third line.

_____   _____   _____
_____   _____   _____
_____   _____   _____
_____   _____   _____
_____   _____   _____

7. Now create a fourth line for your poem. Write your fourth line below.

_____

8. Write your clerihew on the back of this paper. Illustrate it.

ALPHABET POETRY

★ Using the familiar ABC's, poet Paul West has given us alphabet poetry. The traditional arrangement of the ABC's provides the framework for the creative writer who focuses on a particular topic, selects words to capture that topic and arranges the words in ABC order. The final step is the decision about how many words to place on a particular line. Using the strategy suggested for personal poetry (p. 9), some very pleasing free verse can be produced. These poems enjoy a broad range of topic resources and tonal expressions. Here are two examples which focus on some things very common in our environment.

Shoes

Accents, big
clumsy, dirty, elegant
fashionable, grand heels
interesting,
jive, kinky
loafers, messy,
nifty, old, pointy
queer,
ridiculous sneakers
toes up
vamps wide
xceptional, yellow
zany.

Food

Apples
bubbly corn dishes
eating favorites
greedy helpings
ices
juicy kumquat
luscious melons
nuts, oranges, peelings
quiche
ripe strawberries, tacos
unlimited vegetables
weiners
xcellent, yummy zucchini.

When you come to x or z you may use poetic license and form a word that has the sound of the letter in it as in "xcellent" above. You may also create a nonsense word if you are really in trouble.

ALPHABET POETRY

When we select a topic for a poem and use the order of the ABC's for arranging all the words in that poem, we are writing alphabet poetry.

1. Name a topic you wish to explore _____

The topic will become your poem's title.

2. Now think of words which relate to your topic. Be sure you have something for each letter of the alphabet.

A _____	H _____	O _____	V _____
B _____	I _____	P _____	W _____
C _____	J _____	Q _____	X _____
D _____	K _____	R _____	Y _____
E _____	L _____	S _____	Z _____
F _____	M _____	T _____	
G _____	N _____	U _____	

3. Write your ABC poem, using the topic as the title. Follow the ABC's carefully. Pick one word for each letter and keep things in order. Think carefully about how much to place on a line. Separate words with commas. End with a period when necessary.

_____

_____

_____

_____

_____

_____

_____

_____

_____

_____

_____

4. Recopy your poem on a good sheet of paper in your best writing.

ACROSTIC POETRY

★ In an acrostic poem, attention needs to be given to the physical arrangement of the lines on paper. This verse is usually unrhymed. The title of the poem is the subject under consideration. The letters from the title are then rewritten vertically and are used to stimulate creative language thinking about the topic. The skeleton of an acrostic poem looks like this.

Comic Heroes

C _____

O _____

M _____

I _____

C _____

H _____

E _____

R _____

O _____

E _____

S _____

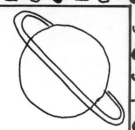

After adequate discussion of the topic, students should then be engaged in generating phrases or short, but effective sentences about the topic. However, the phrases and sentences must begin with the letter appearing vertically.

Once a sufficient number of phrases and statements has been generated, then the selection process begins. Those phrases and statements which, when combined, make the strongest verse are arranged for the final version -- or at least, *one* possible final version. "Comic Heroes" when completed may read,

Comic Heroes
Come one and all to see them fly
Over rooftops winging through space
Many perform great feats of strength
In all manner of athletic styles
Certain to support the cause of goodness.

Home to them is everywhere
Every land is their land
Responding bravely to all in need
Over, above and beyond the virtue of ordinary people
Evil is defeated every time
Splendid creatures every one -- victory is theirs!

G. Lipson

Rock Stars

Ranting and raving
On the stage each night
Collecting screams, cries and
Kisses from adoring groupies

Superstars strutting under flashing lights
Titillating the senses
Assaulting the ears to the
Rocking rhythm--exploding from the
Stage.

G. Lipson

Almost any topic can serve as a fruitful theme for acrostic poetry.

Would any of these be of interest to your students?

politicians
horoscope
teen-ager
computers

birthdays
automobiles
outer space

cheerleaders
movies
dancing

ACROSTIC POETRY

In an acrostic poem the title (topic) is printed vertically, letter by letter. Each letter is used to construct a phrase or sentence which describes the topic.

1. Think of a great movie you have seen or a song you have heard. Write the title here. Short titles work best.

_____

This will be the title of your poem.

2. Now take every letter from your title and write it vertically. Skip a line after each word. Here is a sample.

STAR TREK

S _____

T _____

A _____

R _____

T _____

R _____

E _____

K _____

Now think of a phrase or a statement for each line. Your phrase or sentence must begin with the letter you have placed on the side. All the lines should say something effective about your topic.

_____
(Title)

_____

_____

_____

_____

_____

_____

_____

3. Proofread and edit this poem with your teacher. Recopy it and enter it in a class poetry book.

CINQUAIN

★ Cinquain (sin-cane) is an unrhymed form of poetry consisting of five prescribed lines. Adelaide Crapsey who originated the cinquain form used a syllable formula for writing cinquains. The original form had five lines consisting of syllables arranged in a two, four, six, eight, two-syllable pattern. Adelaide Crapsey's poems were delicate and full of sadness. However, cinquain can be adapted to fit any mood. Here are two examples.

Mantis (2-syllable word or words announcing topic)
Stick predator (4 syllables describing topic)
Stalking, preening, searching (6 syllables expressing action)
Slenderly fashioned by nature (8 syllables expressing feeling)
Killer (2 syllable ending synonym for topic)

G. Lipson

Cinquains, generally, do not bear titles. However, you will notice that the first line serves that function by announcing the topic.

	Syllables
Playground	2
A place to play	4
Boys, girls, teachers, freedom	6
Free my spirit--send me flying	8
Hooray!	2

G. Lipson

A variation of the cinquain focuses on topics not normally used for cinquain. These topics can cut across all curriculum areas. Your students may be interested in writing cinquains which focus on:

famous modern women
a great moment in history or modern times
a scientific phenomenon
a fascinating title of a book or movie
a social issue
a mathematical concept

We need to make account here of a version of cinquain which is quite popular in the schools but which does not observe the syllabic pattern devised by Adelaide Crapsey. Many teachers find this pattern easier for less sophisticated poetry writers. It consists of the following:

_____ one-word topic (noun)

_____ _____ two describing words (adjectives)

_____ _____ _____ three action words (verbs)

_____ a four-word phrase

_____ a synonym or equivalent for the topic (noun)

An example of this cinquain pattern would be:

Rain

Heavy, awesome

Drenching, soaking, penetrating

Renewing the earth's firmament

Soil-soaker

J. Romatowski

CINQUAIN

Cinquain is a form of free verse consisting of five lines arranged in a very special way. If you follow the directions below, you will have written a cinquain of your own.

1. Name a topic _____

2. Think of describing words for your topic.

    _____   _____   _____   _____

    _____   _____   _____   _____

3. Think of "ing" action words that fit your topic.

    _____   _____   _____   _____

    _____   _____   _____   _____

4. Now think of some four-word phrases which capture some feeling about your topic.

    _____

    _____

    _____

    _____

    _____

5. How many synonyms can you think of for your topic? Use hyphenated words or a strong emotional word if you prefer.

    _____   _____   _____   _____

    _____   _____   _____   _____

6.   Pick out your best words and put your cinquain together, below. Cut it out and mount it on construction paper. Do your best writing. Remember the pattern -- the first line is 2 syllables, second line 4 syllables, third line 6 syllables, fourth line 8 syllables, fifth line 2 syllables.

_____
1.

_____,   _____
2.

_____,   _____,   _____
3.

_____
4.

_____
5.

By: _____

DIAMANTE

★ A "kissin' cousin" of the cinquain is the form of unrhymed poetry created by Iris Tiedt, labeled diamante. Because its physical appearance on paper resembles that of a diamond, it was christened with the Italian word for diamond--diamante. This poem is more symmetrical in looks and sound, yet the same teaching technique used for cinquain can be used to teach diamante. Though it allows for flexibility and adaptation, the two simplest forms of diamante appear below.

Pattern I

topic (noun)
two describing words (adjectives)
three action words (verbs or "ing" action words)
a four-word phrase capturing some feeling about the topic
three action words (verbs or "ing" words)
two describing words (adjectives)
ending word (noun, synonym, strong emotional word
or hyphenated word for the topic)

Here is an example of diamante, Pattern I.

Peace
Joyful, free
Caring, sharing, forgiving
World fellowship and brotherhood
Lasting, abiding, never-ending
Quiet, serene
Tranquility

Pattern II - Using Opposites

It must be noted that when Pattern II (using opposites) is being explored, the teacher must work from both ends but one line at a time. That means the development will be as shown at the top of the next page .

1. Name the topic noun (first line).
2. Decide on the antonym (last line).
3. Select two describing words for topic noun.
4. Select two describing words for antonym.
5. Generate three action words for topic noun.
6. Generate three action words for antonym.
7. Decide on four words (nouns are best) two of which fit the topic noun and two of which fit the antonym, ending noun.

topic (noun)

two describing words (adjectives)

three action words (verbs or "ing" action words)

Two words to capture topic noun   two words to capture ending noun

three action words for ending noun

two describing words for ending noun

ending noun: antonym (opposite of topic word)

Here are some samples of diamante poems, Pattern II:

LOVE

Warm, wonderful

Embracing, hugging, laughing

Parents, relatives, -- Strangers, enemies

Neglected, frightened, trembling,

Cold, bitter,

Hate   G. Lipson

FOOD

Fresh, crisp

Simmering, cooking, nourishing

Delicacies, appetizers, -- Leftovers, scraps

Chewing, softening, absorbing

Remnants, discards

Garbage

G. Lipson

Some interesting opposing ideas to use for writing diamante in Pattern II would be:

city - country
clean - dirty
young - old
fat - thin
truth - lies
dark - light
pleasure - pain
hungry - full
midget - giant
failure - success
weak - strong
ice - water

A variation of diamante with which we have had fun in classrooms as well as teacher workshops involves the use of an ordinary object (a pencil, a sheet of paper, paper towel rolls, etc.). The class is asked to imagine another use for the object. The word for the imagined use becomes the last word in the diamante while the actual object is the first word. Other lines are developed as usual. Here is a sample:

Pencil
Long, slender
Writing, drawing, sketching
Creating glorious memorable moments
Waving, directing, conducting
Shiny, slim
Baton

J Romatowski

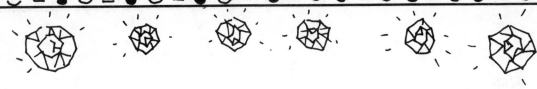

A SPARKLING DIAMANTE

Here is an opportunity for you to create a diamante. If you follow the directions below carefully, you will have a good collection of words and phrases to use for your poem.

1. Choose a topic. _____
                                      (one word)

2. Name describing words for your topic.

    _____   _____   _____

    _____   _____   _____

3. Name some action words for your topic. Verbs ending in "ing" are helpful.

    _____   _____   _____

    _____   _____   _____

    _____   _____   _____

4. Write some four-word phrases which capture a feeling about your topic.

    _____

    _____

    _____

5. Choose an ending word for your poem. _____
                                                      (synonym)

- -

Select your favorites from the work sheet above to create your own diamante.

1. topic   _____

2. two adjectives   _____   _____

3. three action words   _____   _____   _____

4. one phrase   _____

5. three action words   _____   _____   _____

6. two adjectives   _____   _____

7. synonym   _____

HAIKU

★ From the Japanese we have inherited the sensitive yet powerful haiku (high-coo). The haiku is a three-line, seventeen syllable, unrhymed (usually) poem which uses nature as its primary focus. There are numerous collections of haiku translated from the Japanese as well as those created by English writers. Some are exquisitely illustrated. It would be very simple to arrange an entire unit of study around Japanese culture and art (especially the pen and ink drawings). Haiku books are readily available at any public library. You may have some in the school's resource center or library, also.

The haiku, it has been said, captures a moment in nature or in life and freezes it with disciplined language. Each reader, then, thaws the message, the picture painted by words, and brings the scene to life.

We have found that upper elementary grade students are the most capable of working with the haiku. Younger students tend to stay too literal, too concrete. The clever thing about the haiku is its ability to convey a mood or a feeling through the picture painted in words. Explicit language denoting feeling is not generally used. Consider these samples:

> An old silent pond (5)
> A frog jumps into the pond (7)
> Splash, silence again. (5)
> > Basho
>
> In the darkest woods (5)
> A weeping willow tree cries (7)
> Who made such sadness? (5)
> > G. Lipson

Without telling us so, each poem not only captures a moment in nature, but clearly conveys a mood, a tone.

Though we have simplified a good deal, you will find that your students can generate some sensitive haiku, if you,

1) keep the focus on nature
2) help the students generate colorful phrases
3) assist with the syllabication of each phrase
4) practice writing haiku sufficiently with the entire class before expecting individual effort.

An approach that we have used repeatedly and which has not failed us is as follows:

1. Engage the class in a discussion of the season. Allow them to reflect on scenes that come to their minds and share with the class.

2. Now, ask each student to "zero-in" on *one* spot in his scene. Can he give you a picturesque phrase to capture that spot? When you are given a rather ordinary phrase, ask the student to "stretch" it so that others can sense the picture more clearly. You want to move, for example, from "a lake" to "a lazy, placid lake," etc.

3. Brainstorm for phrases and fill your chalkboard with as many as you can. (Do not deal with syllabication at this point.) Leave one section of the chalkboard free for the creation of the haiku, later.

4. *Now*, review each phrase for syllabication. Placing check marks above the syllables helps. When there are too many or too few syllables, make adjustments immediately so that the phrase is either a 5-syllable or a 7-syllable phrase. For example,

> a lazy, placid lake (6 syllables)
> can be changed to
> lazy, placid lake (5 syllables)

or to

> lazy, placid, moon-filled lake (7 syllables).

5. When all phrases have been marked for syllable content, ask one student to select a 5-syllable phrase that would make a good starter for painting a word picture.

6. Read the phrase to the class. Ask them to reflect on it and then to select a 7-syllable phrase that preserves meaning and tone. Write it as the second line of the haiku.

7. Complete the poem with the selection of a 5-syllable phrase for the third line.

HAIKU

Haiku is a three-line poem of Japanese origin which usually focuses on nature. It is not ordinarily a rhyming poem, but it does pay careful attention to syllables.

1. Look through a magazine and find a nature scene that is special. Cut it out and mount it on construction paper.

2. Sit quietly and look deeply into your picture. Think about all the interesting ways to describe the scene.

3. Write at least 10 - 12 colorful phrases which capture the mood and the picture.

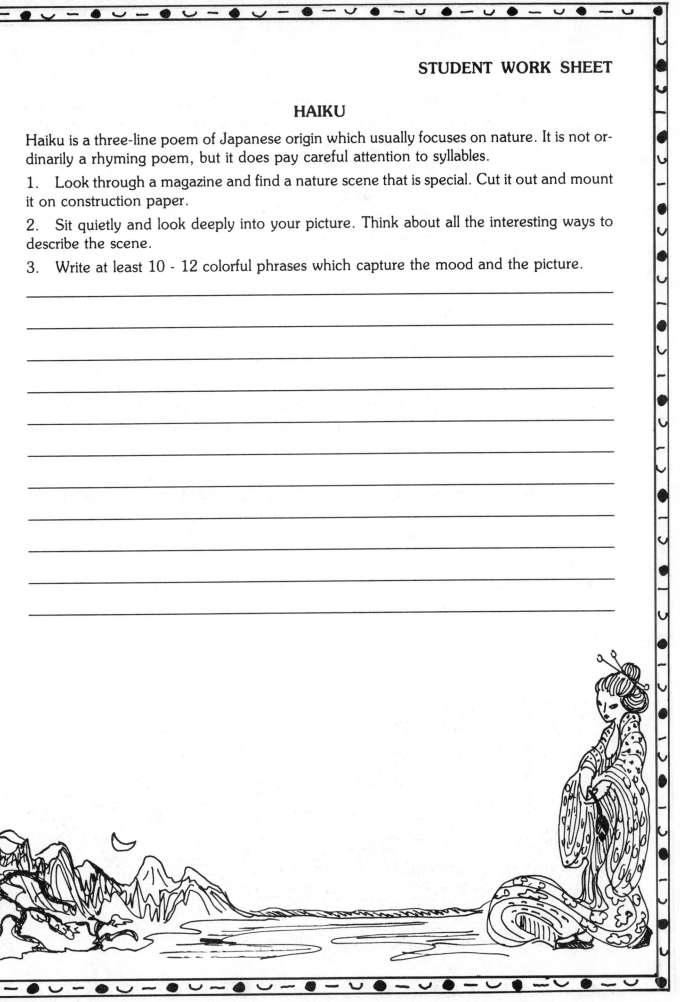

4.   Check the syllables to be sure that each phrase is either 5 syllables or 7 syllables long.

5.   Select a 5-syllable phrase which makes the best starter. Write it as line one, below.

_____

6.   Now pick a 7-syllable phrase that keeps the meaning and mood you started in the first line. Write it as line two, below.

_____

7.   For your third line, pick a 5-syllable phrase which ends your haiku in a satisfactory way.

_____

8.   Proofread and edit your haiku, rewrite it below and paste it below your picture.

_____

_____

_____

_____

_____

_____

_____

TANKA

★ Very similar to haiku, only longer, is the form of Japanese verse called tanka. It consists of a total of 31 syllables distributed in the following way:

Line 1 . . . . .5 syllables
Line 2 . . . . .7 syllables
Line 3 . . . . .5 syllables
Line 4 . . . . .7 syllables
Line 5 . . . . .7 syllables

You will notice that the first three lines are identical to haiku. The procedures used for writing tanka are the same as those for haiku. It would be important, however, to have more 7-syllable phrases generated and available on the chalkboard for use in creating tanka.

An interesting class activity is to pair children off and have the partnerships write only the first three lines of the tanka. When the task is completed by everyone, collect the three-liners.

Redistribute so that no partnership has its own paper. Now, invite students to reflect on the three-liners before them and to complete them with the last two lines, each being a 7-syllable line.

Return the tankas to the original owners. Have a sharing session and make positive acknowledgment of the creative effort revealed in the writing of tanka. Using appropriate background music, these tankas lend themselves well to dramatic reading. The tapes can then be used as an accompaniment to a slide show featuring relevant scenes.

Two samples of a tanka follow:

	Syllables
The rain spills from clouds	(5)
Over thirsty grass and trees	(7)
It mists the landscape	(5)
Like a soft gentle shower	(7)
Spring awakens the whole world.	(7)
G. Lipson	
Warm us today sun	(5)
Come look down with your hot smile	(7)
We'll look up at you	(5)
And worship your gift to us	(7)
Yellow ball gives growth and joy.	(7)
G. Lipson	

TANKA

Tanka is a poem of Japanese origin consisting of 31 syllables distributed across five lines. This poetic form does not usually rhyme.

1.   Think of a scenic spot or gaze out the classroom window, quietly.

2.   Capture in words what you see and feel. Write as many colorful phrases as you can think of.

_____

_____

_____

_____

_____

_____

_____

_____

_____

_____

_____

3.   Check each phrase. Adjust your phrases until all are either 7 or 5 syllables long.

4.   Now, create a tanka below, cut it out and mount it for display.

_____

(5 syllables)

_____

(7 syllables)

_____

(5 syllables)

_____

(7 syllables)

_____

(7 syllables)

By: _____

COUPLETS -- SMART TWO-LINERS

★ The binding together of two things, as in a pair, can be called a couplet. And so in verse writing, a couplet is a verse composed of two lines (length of line depends on the writer) and most typically appearing in rhymed fashion. Couplets can be simple or sophisticated.

But if the while I think on thee, dear friend,   a
All losses are restored and sorrows end.   a

Shakespeare

The world is so full of a number of things   a
I'm sure we should all be as happy as kings   a

Robert Louis Stevenson

Creative writers have enjoyed the discipline of capturing an idea in a couplet. At times, a writer will use a series of couplets to construct one poem. In the classroom, such poems can be easily constructed when the teacher helps the class to focus on a particular theme, for example, sports and sport phrases. After enough have been generated and the chalkboard is full, the class can be encouraged to construct a possible first line. It might be:

I started to race with the rest of the pack

Now, brainstorm for a list of words that rhyme with "pack." List all contributions on the board. Have your class now construct a second line which keeps the same rhythm. The only way to assure this is to read and reread aloud different endings together with the first line. Make adjustments by adding or deleting a word or a syllable until the rhythm is right. Write the final version on the board. It may be:

I started to race with the rest of the pack
Though my lungs are on fire I won't turn back!

G. Lipson

Construct several of these couplets with your class. For fun, place a starter line-- or several -- on the chalkboard. Have your students work in pairs to find as many rhyming words as they can for each ending word. Have the lists read out loud. Now, using the lists and all the shared words, construct as many second lines as possible for the starter line. The teacher should be the scribe and fill the board with the contributions. This is a good way to build student confidence in writing, but especially in rhyming. Some starter lines with a possible completion (in parentheses) appear below.

Take my nice, new shiny nickel
(Sell me that juicy, garlic pickle)!

His mustache looks like a bushy wig
(He likes it that way 'cause his nose is big).

He's smart and he's slicker
(But I'm really quicker).

You'll love my granny
(She's really uncanny).

I like this story
(It isn't too gory)!

G. Lipson

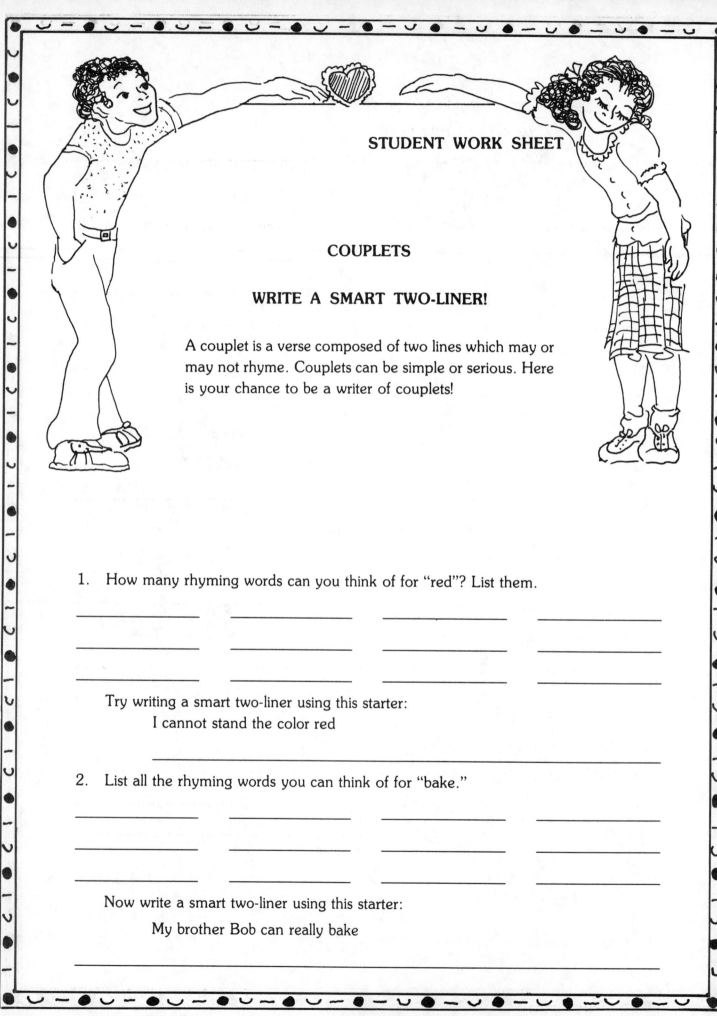

COUPLETS

WRITE A SMART TWO-LINER!

A couplet is a verse composed of two lines which may or may not rhyme. Couplets can be simple or serious. Here is your chance to be a writer of couplets!

1. How many rhyming words can you think of for "red"? List them.

_____ _____ _____ _____

_____ _____ _____ _____

_____ _____ _____ _____

Try writing a smart two-liner using this starter:
    I cannot stand the color red

    _____

2. List all the rhyming words you can think of for "bake."

_____ _____ _____ _____

_____ _____ _____ _____

_____ _____ _____ _____

Now write a smart two-liner using this starter:

    My brother Bob can really bake

    _____

3. Can you think of a beautiful two-liner? Try this starter:

>   Don't be sad on this fine day

>   _____

Now, try writing couplets of your own. They can be beautiful, funny, clever, sad, or witty.

_____

_____

_____

_____

_____

_____

_____

_____

_____

_____

_____

TRIPLETS -- SNAPPY THREE-LINERS

★ The triplet, though not as common as the couplet (two-liner) or the quatrain (four-liner), nevertheless, can be an exciting, creative writing experience. The triplet, or tercet as it is sometimes called, can be either rhymed or unrhymed. When rhymed it allows for a variety of rhyming patterns aaa, aab, aba, abb. The haiku, discussed earlier, which is usually written unrhymed, is a good example of the triplet. The triplet can be simple or complex.

Higher than a house,	a
Higher than a tree,	b
Oh! Whatever can that be?	b

Mother Goose

We have fallen in the dreams the ever-living	a
Breathe on the tarnished mirror of the world,	b
And then smooth out with ivory hands and sigh.	c

W. B. Yeats

The lines of a triplet can be the same length or they may differ in length. They can reflect beautiful thoughts or ordinary events. Here are some examples.

Buddies			New Year's Eve	
My friend is mad	a		Family and friends are we	a
He wouldn't play	b		Celebration and merriment to see	a
Instead he only ran away.	b		Why, does it always trouble me?	a

G. Lipson   J. Romatowski

Rover			Blind Love	
I mourn my dog.	a		Minute by minute, hour by hour	a
I'm not ashamed	b		The sun penetrates the growing flower	a
To say I loved him.	c		Leading it to its inevitable end.	b

G. Lipson   J. Romatowski

Awakening	
The presents that you bring	a
Are not only just for me	b
Because you brought the spring.	a

G. Lipson

TRIPLETS
SNAPPY THREE-LINERS

Triplets are three-line poems which can rhyme in a variety of ways. Try your hand at some of the incomplete triplets written below.

 1. Each triplet (snappy three-liner) has one line missing. Can you write one that fits the meaning of the poem and keeps its rhythm? Follow the rhyming pattern for each triplet below.

The waiter hollered down the hall	a)	
_____	a)	All three lines rhyme
He carried one meat ball	a)	
Autumn leaves fall	a)	
To the ground below	b)	The first and last lines rhyme
_____a	)	
Comb your hair!	a)	
It's out of place	b)	The last two lines rhyme
_____b	)	

Write your own triplets below, cut them out, mount them and display.

_____

_____

_____

_____

_____

_____

_____

_____

_____

QUATRAINS -- FANCY FOUR-LINERS

★ The name of this poetic form is a clue to its structure. A quart equals four cups, a quadrangle has four angles and four sides, and a quarter portion is a fourth of something. A quatrain, then, is a poem written in four lines --rhymed or unrhymed. When rhymed, it allows for a variety of rhyming patterns, such as aa bb, ab ab, ab cb, aaaa, etc. Quatrains are extremely common in verse writing. It would be fun to have your class make a library search for quatrains and to construct individual books of their favorites.

Quatrains, like triplets and couplets, can be simple or complex with a variety of rhyming patterns. They can reflect ordinary events in life, silly musings, or profound thoughts.

He tossed the pizza oh so high	a
Over his head, up toward the sky	a
My stomach churned with sheer disgust	b
To see the pizza hit the dust.	b

G. Lipson

I had a very nasty scheme	a
I dreamed it in a wicked dream	a
To point my trusty laser beam	a
And turn the villains all to steam.	a

G. Lipson

Hippety hop to the barber shop	a
To get a stick of candy,	b
One for you and one for me,	c
And one for Sister Mandy.	b

Mother Goose

After much reading and sharing of quatrains, it is a good idea to place three or four on the chalkboard for purposes of examining the rhyming pattern in each. It would be unwise to subject the poems to such scrutiny before the enjoyment of quatrains is well settled-in. Once examined, students can look in their own books of favorites to see if they can find quatrains which match the pattern discussed. These can be read and enjoyed by the entire class.

Now practice writing quatrains with the entire class. When enough practice has been achieved, some small group activity would be in order. Begin by giving each small group the same starting line. Allow for sufficient work time. When the quatrains are complete, allow groups to present their quatrains to the rest of the class. Highlight colorful phrases, sensitive thoughts, clever endings, rhyming patterns and catchy titles. Be positive. Demonstrate your enjoyment of the writing effort. Compile class books of these original quatrains!

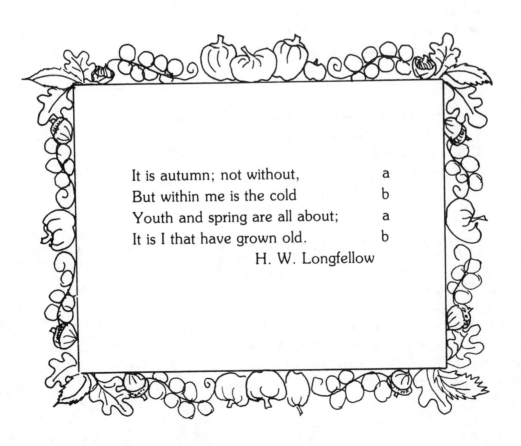

It is autumn; not without,   a
But within me is the cold   b
Youth and spring are all about;   a
It is I that have grown old.   b

H. W. Longfellow

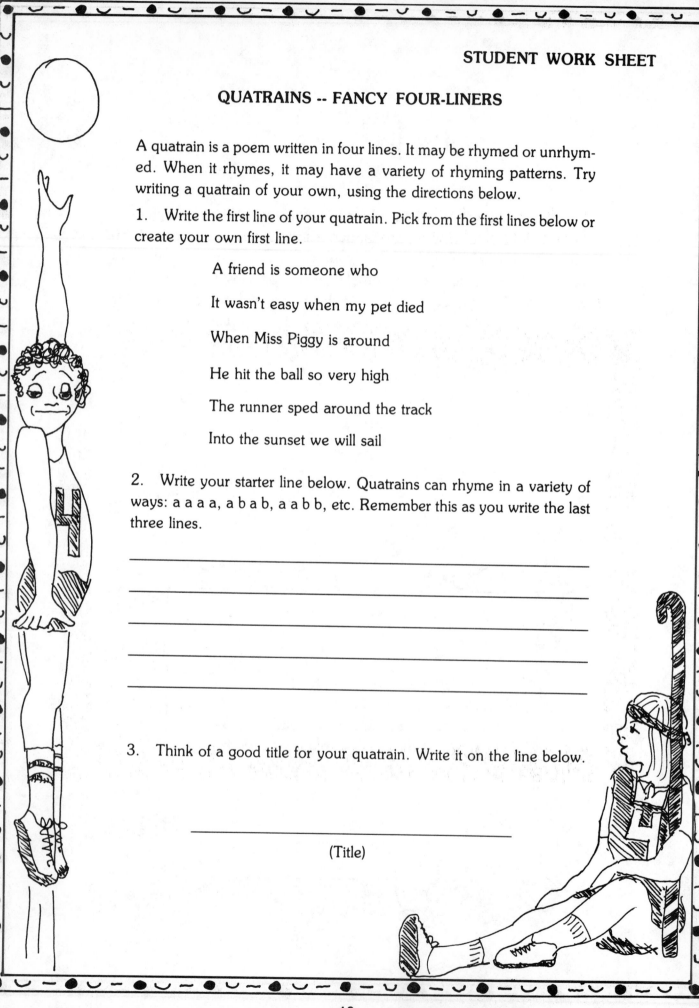

QUATRAINS -- FANCY FOUR-LINERS

A quatrain is a poem written in four lines. It may be rhymed or unrhymed. When it rhymes, it may have a variety of rhyming patterns. Try writing a quatrain of your own, using the directions below.

1. Write the first line of your quatrain. Pick from the first lines below or create your own first line.

> A friend is someone who
>
> It wasn't easy when my pet died
>
> When Miss Piggy is around
>
> He hit the ball so very high
>
> The runner sped around the track
>
> Into the sunset we will sail

2. Write your starter line below. Quatrains can rhyme in a variety of ways: a a a a, a b a b, a a b b, etc. Remember this as you write the last three lines.

_____

_____

_____

_____

_____

3. Think of a good title for your quatrain. Write it on the line below.

_____

(Title)

4. Now write the final version of your quatrain below. Cut it out, and decorate it for display or for your poetry book.

_____
(Title)

_____

_____

_____

_____

By : _____

SONNETS

★ For those *sophisticated* writers in your class seeking more of a writing challenge, the sonnet may be the answer. A word of caution -- the sonnet is a specialized and disciplined form of poetry. It may be best used in the classroom as a listening experience only. However, sonnets can be written by the entire class, as a group experience, with an informed teacher as a guide. The English sonnet, sometimes called the Shakespearean sonnet, will relate best to previous poetry writing.

This lyric poem consists of 14 lines -- as do all sonnets -- but arranged as three quatrains and a couplet. *The quatrains usually establish the idea, or the problem, while the couplet usually serves as a summary statement, a final comment, or a philosophical stance.*

More important than any other factor in an overall teaching strategy for sonnets will be the reading of sonnets to your class and the reading of sonnets by your students. Activities such as library searches for favorite sonnets to memorize and recite or making a personal book of well-liked sonnets will also be helpful. Once the experience with sonnets has been well established, the teacher can then proceed to the group activities for writing.

Once your class has been writing quatrains, it is easy to move toward one focus and to help the class write three quatrains on that focus and then a final couplet. And there is the sonnet! The rhyming pattern in sonnets is important and children will need to know that. The rhyming formula of a sonnet appears at the top of the next page.

_____	a	
_____	b	quatrain
_____	a	
_____	b	
_____	c	
_____	d	quatrain
_____	c	
_____	d	
_____	e	
_____	f	quatrain
_____	e	
_____	f	
_____	g	
_____	g	couplet

Meter, or beat (the measurement of a poetic line by rhythmic feet), is also important, but our feeling is that developing an inner ear for rhythm is more important at the elementary and middle school level than an understanding of iambic pentameter. High school is early enough for such refinements.

It should be noted that the study and writing of sonnets need not be a whole class project. It may be the better part of wisdom to offer such an opportunity on an invitational basis only. Those students who are *interested* can form a "Sonneteers' Club" while others pursue interests in other curriculum areas. Given the developmental levels of the children who would be capable of such writing, *the matter of choice* would be dear to a student's heart. Having some control over one's environment is very important to students.

A simple way to acknowledge the skill of your classroom sonnet *writers* is to present them with a certificate of membership in the "Sonneteers' Club." A second certificate of membership in the club is provided for those students who demonstrate an *appreciation* of the sonnet form. Models for each type of membership are provided as Student Work Sheets.

Sonnets can be reflections on life's ordinary events, on poignant moments in life, on burning issues, on love's adventures. They can be light in tone or quite dramatic. When exposing your class to listening experiences, select sonnets to represent such a range of tone and interest.

Here is a sonnet you alone or you and your students may enjoy.

Shall I compare thee to a summer's day?
Thou art more lovely and more temperate:
Rough winds do shake the darling buds of May,
And summer's lease hath all too short a date:

Sometime too hot the eye of heaven shines,
And often is his gold complexion dimm'd;
And every fair from fair sometime declines,
By chance or nature's changing course untrimm'd:

But thy eternal summer shall not fade
Nor lose possession of that fair thou ow'st;
Nor shall Death brag thou wanderest in his shade,
When in eternal lines to time thou grow'st;

So long as men can breath or eyes can see,
So long lives this and this gives life to thee.

W. Shakespeare

The Quadrangle: Sixteenth Street, Marquette, Linwood, and McGraw
A Sonnet of the City

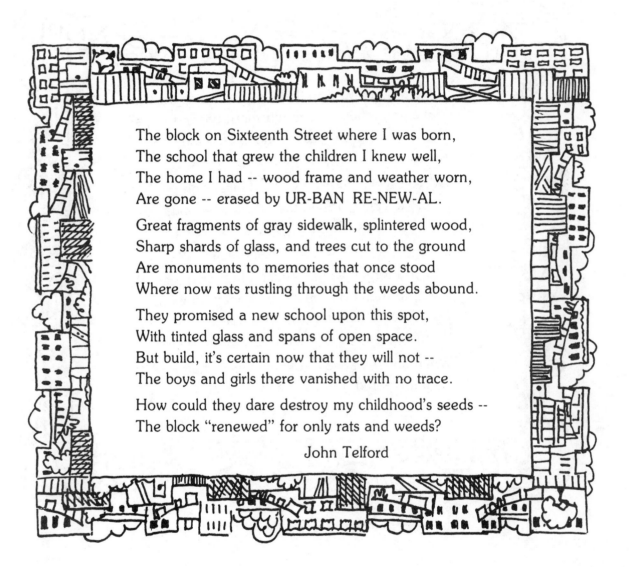

The block on Sixteenth Street where I was born,
The school that grew the children I knew well,
The home I had -- wood frame and weather worn,
Are gone -- erased by UR-BAN RE-NEW-AL.

Great fragments of gray sidewalk, splintered wood,
Sharp shards of glass, and trees cut to the ground
Are monuments to memories that once stood
Where now rats rustling through the weeds abound.

They promised a new school upon this spot,
With tinted glass and spans of open space.
But build, it's certain now that they will not --
The boys and girls there vanished with no trace.

How could they dare destroy my childhood's seeds --
The block "renewed" for only rats and weeds?

John Telford

I heard that you were back in our hometown.
Have you reflected through these passing years?
We were the very best of friends around.
Emotions roil to comtemplate you near.

Do you feel pain from our old bitter fight?
I can't decide who did the grievous wrong,
Or who it was whose cause was in the right
Nor did it matter much, once you were gone.

Will you forget we gave each other grief?--
I wish to mend our breach in hopeful dreams
To still regret and give my soul relief
Be mine again, dear friend, in healing scenes.

When anger waned -- I knew what I had lost
So unprepared was I to pay the cost.

Greta B. Lipson

CERTIFICATE OF MEMBERSHIP

in the

SONNETEERS' CLUB

_____ is awarded

(Student's name)

membership in the Sonneteers' Club on this

the _____ day of _____, in the

year _____, for WRITING the original sonnet
which appears below.

_____

(Title)

_____

_____

_____

_____

_____

_____

_____

_____

_____

_____

_____

_____

_____

_____

By: _____

_____

(Teacher's signature)

CERTIFICATE OF MEMBERSHIP

in the

SONNETEERS' CLUB

_____ is awarded membership in

(Student's name)

the Sonneteers' Club on this the _____ day of _____,

in the year _____. This certificate acknowledges the

member's APPRECIATION of the sonnet form. The member's

favorite sonnet appears below.

_____

(Title)

_____

_____

_____

_____

_____

_____

_____

_____

_____

_____

_____

_____

_____

Poet: _____

_____

(Teacher's signature)

CONCRETE AND VISUAL POETRY

★ Though it does have historical roots, concrete poetry has enjoyed attention only within the last twenty-five years or so. This attention runs parallel with developments in "pop" art, in impressionistic photography, in graphics, architecture, etc. The most common type of concrete poetry depends on incorporating an array of poetically pleasing words or phrases with a strong visual component which identifies the topic in some way. For example, a three-liner such as:

> Large blackbirds
> Peppering the sky,
> Announce autumn.
>
> J. Romatowski

would be teamed up with a visual component (blackbirds) and would look like this perhaps:

Another three-liner,

> The sands of time
> Drip relentlessly
> With clear finality.
>
> J. Romatowski

may be arranged cleverly within an hour glass, for example,

The visual impact is meant to enhance the enjoyment of the sensitive lines.

It would be a good idea to prepare your class for the writing of concrete poetry with related activities. Proverbs, the idioms of our language, sayings, and even words alone can serve as starting points. Using words with strong visual appeal, can you and your students make words look like their meanings? For example:

Try these with your class:

flag	eye
tall	tear (as in crying)
small	wide
wide	stretch
lightning	explode

New and old idioms also lend themselves to such concrete forms. For example:

CONCRETE AND VISUAL POETRY
ILLUSTRATING THE LANGUAGE

If we think about it, we know that there are certain words and sayings in our language which easily suggest pictures in our minds. Explore some of these words and sayings with pictures.

Part I.   WORD PICTURES

Here is an illustration of a word that captures the word's meaning –

Look

Can you do the same for these words:

drip   fraction

break   chair

zigzag   nervous

Part II.   SENTENCE PICTURES

Pick a saying you like. Underline it.

Far out!   Go, soak your head.

It's raining cats and dogs.   You hit the nail right on the head.

Drop in sometime!   You're right on target!

Now, illustrate the saying in the box below. Don't worry about the intended meaning. Use the words in their ordinary senses. Your illustration will be silly, of course, when compared to the actual meaning intended. Write the saying you have selected below your illustration.

CONCRETE AND VISUAL POETRY
WRITE A CONCRETE POEM

Concrete poetry is a combination of poetic language arranged in the shape of the topic being considered. Here are two examples.

BUTTERFLIES   THE FOOTBALL

1. Think of a topic about which you would like to write a concrete poem. Remember that the topic you choose must be one that can be illustrated! Write the topic here. _____

2. Now think of *poetic* words and phrases for your topic.

_____   _____

_____   _____

_____   _____

_____   _____

_____   _____

3. Select those words or phrases which are best and most poetic sounding. Below, lightly design the shape of your topic. Write in the phrases and words you have selected. Be careful with the arrangement. The reader will depend on you to arrange the words in such a way that they can be easily read.

SOUND POETRY

★ Using the senses for writing poetry is a useful technique. Our sense of hearing, for example, can provide much input for writing verse--especially free verse. By capitalizing on the sound environment at hand, students can be encouraged to concentrate on listening to sounds. Each sound can be recorded on lined paper in a colorful phrase or sentence. The phrase or sentence should not exceed the physical limitations of one line of the paper. We have found that this helps with rhythm to a certain degree. When a number of such sound impressions are gathered (8 to 10 suffice), then the student is asked to quietly read and reread the writing for the purpose of placing the statements in the best, most pleasing order. When the ordering has been decided, the statements are numbered for easy reading, and an oral sharing session can ensue. The teacher should participate also and can be the first volunteer in the oral reading of sound poetry.

In addition to the classroom and the immediate area outside the classroom windows, you may find inspiration for verse writing by taking your class to:

1. A quiet nature trail
2. The cafeteria
3. The hallway
4. The library
5. The airport
6. The supermarket
7. The football practice field
8. The principal's office
9. The playground
10. The school boiler room
11. The corner (for street sounds)
12. The shopping mall

The writing of sound poetry is good work for a small group activity, especially three in a group. The plan recommended earlier for collecting sound impressions on paper should be observed. The class should then be grouped into triads. The tasks in each triad would be:

1. Have each person in the group read all the written sound impressions they have recorded.

2. The group will select the three best impressions from each person's paper.

3. Each person in the triad will write his three sound impressions on separate slips of paper.

4. The threesome will arrange and rearrange the lines until a pleasing order is achieved.

5. A title will be selected.

6. The lines will be proofread and edited.

7. Each person will write the finished sound poem on fresh paper.

8. The poem will be signed by each poet in the triad.

These poems make a strong impression when read aloud. Plan to allow time in your classroom for such sharing.

Here are some samples of sound poetry.

Street Sounds

The whizzing of a motor bike charging down the street
A clinking garbage can lid
Somewhere a buzz saw is working
Kids shouting and shooting baskets on the drive
A baby's cry floats out the window
The wind rustles the trees overhead
My mother's voice calls me.

G. Lipson

The Game

Chattering from the players
Stones kicked on the gravel
Balls whipped into mitts
Yelling back and forth from the bleachers
A bat cracks the ball
The umpire shouts his decision
My team groans.

G. Lipson

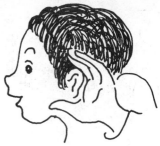

SOUND POETRY

Can You Hear a Poem?

Sound poetry is created by listening to sounds and recording those sound impressions on paper in a pleasing order.

1. Find a good listening location.

2. Listen carefully. Closing your eyes may help you concentrate on the sounds. Do this for at least three minutes.

3. Now, select one sound at a time to concentrate on. Think of a colorful way to capture what you hear in words.

4. Write your phrase or statement down on line one. Keep to one line only.

5. Now, concentrate on a second sound. Capture it in words. Write it on the second line.

6. Continue doing this until you have recorded ten sound impressions.

_____

_____

_____

_____

_____

_____

_____

_____

_____

_____

7. Look carefully through your list. Check the eight statements you like best. Proofread and edit them. Make each statement sparkling clear.

8. Take a fresh sheet of paper or use the back of this one and rewrite your poem. You may want to rearrange the order of your lines until you decide on the most pleasing poetic sound.

9. Give your poem a title and be sure to sign your name as poet.

GENERAL INSTRUCTIONS

PLAY CHANTS

★ Play chants have been around for as long as children have played games. Such chants help keep the rhythm when skipping rope, bouncing balls, or hopscotching on the sidewalk. You will discover that your students can contribute well when you launch the discussion of play chants. Encourage them to share such chants and encourage clapping out the rhythm to the chant. Enjoy saying them aloud together as in choral reading. As the teacher, share some chants you remember from your own childhood. What a pleasant "humanizing" experience for students to realize that their teachers were once boys and girls, too!

Some chants have stood the test of time and are still used--sometimes with modification--by children today. How many of the following chants do you recognize? Do your students recognize them? Have some been adapted? Are there newer versions?

A. One potato, two potato,
    Three potato, four;
    Five potato, six potato,
    Seven potato, *MORE*.

B. Johnnie over the ocean,
    Johnnie over the sea,
    Johnnie broke a milk bottle,
    And blamed it on me.
    I told Ma,
    Ma told Pa,
    Johnnie got a spankin'
    Ha! Ha! Ha!

C. I love my papa, that I do,
    And mama says she loves him, too,
    But papa says he fears some day,
    With some bad man I'll run away.

D. Little Miss Pink,
   Dressed in blue
   Died last night
   At quarter past two.
   Before she died
   She told me this:
   When I jump rope
   I always miss.

E. One-a-larry
   Two-a-larry
   Three-a-larry - four,
   Five-a-larry
   Six-a-larry
   Seven-a-larry more!

F. One for the money
   Two for the show
   Three to get ready
   And four to go!

The enjoyment of such chants could be the plan for one day's exploration. Perhaps you can get volunteers to carefully write up the chants for display. When displayed in the hall, they would provide interesting reading fare for the whole school.

Encourage your students to interview other family members for chants. These can be shared in class, also. There may be some interesting regional or cultural variations to the chants. Such variations can spark an interesting discussion on the dynamic nature of language itself.

With your students, it may be interesting to select *one* chant and as a whole group experience write a parody on it or write additional verses to the chant. Here is an additional verse for "One for the money..."

Five for the ladies,
Six for the men,
Seven to get finished,
And eight to win!

This may be a parody for "Johnnie over the ocean..."

Johnnie over the rooftop
Johnnie over the tree.
Johnnie ate the cookies,
And blamed it on me!

I told Ma,
Ma told Pa,
Johnnie got grounded,
Ha, ha, ha!

Small groups (2 to 3) may enjoy selecting a chant and writing an additional verse or a parody on it. These chants can then be used for choral reading presentations in other classes. They can also be written on poster board and hung below the original chant. If displayed in the hallway of the school, as earlier suggested, you will find other students in the school reading them with interest and enjoyment.

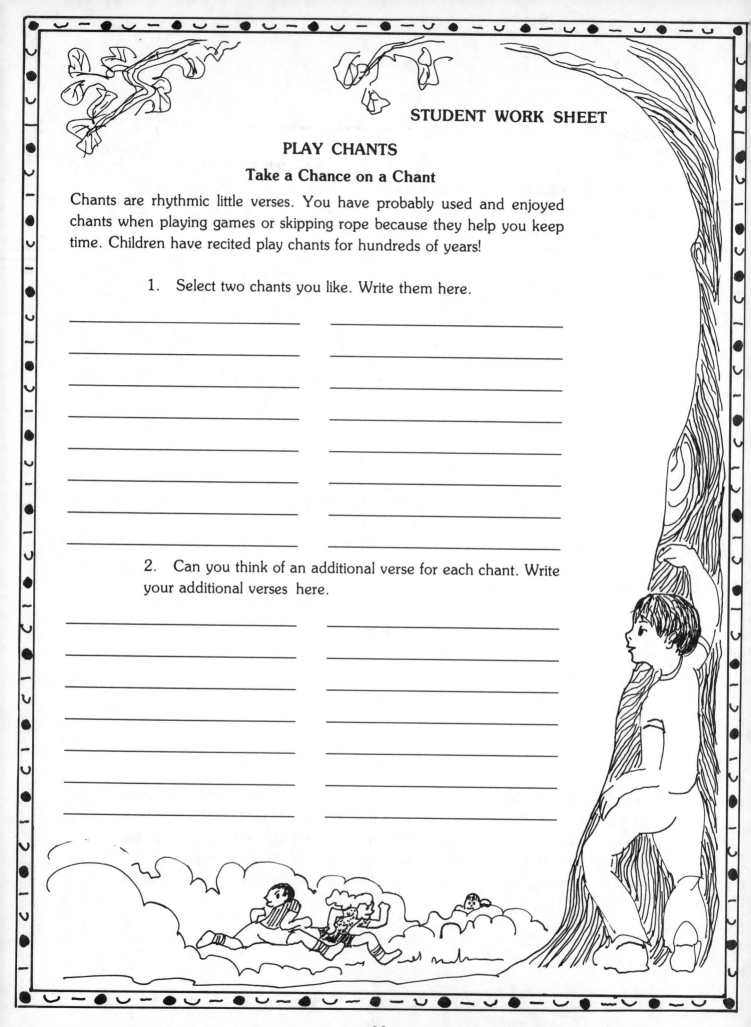

STUDENT WORK SHEET

PLAY CHANTS

Take a Chance on a Chant

Chants are rhythmic little verses. You have probably used and enjoyed chants when playing games or skipping rope because they help you keep time. Children have recited play chants for hundreds of years!

1. Select two chants you like. Write them here.

_____   _____
_____   _____
_____   _____
_____   _____
_____   _____
_____   _____
_____   _____

2. Can you think of an additional verse for each chant. Write your additional verses here.

_____   _____
_____   _____
_____   _____
_____   _____
_____   _____
_____   _____

GENERAL INSTRUCTIONS

BALLADS

★ Folk ballads are simple narrative poems (stories) which may be sung. They can be effectively rendered through recitation, also. A cursory glance at ballads, young and old, reveals quickly that they seem to focus on major issues in life: birth, death; on historical events; on issues of social justice; on heroes and heroines (real and fictional). Because of this, they lend themselves well to creative writing in today's classroom. The classroom teacher can integrate the study of ballads and the writing of ballads with many social studies units, with the study of biography, with the study of tall tales, legends, fairy tales, etc. The possibilities are numerous.

A good starting point for the study of ballads is the study of pop songs where -- in the lyrics -- substantial issues are raised. An examination of such songs can lead to a study of ballads, generally. Librarians and the children are good resource people for gathering a collection of songbooks and record albums.

By using the music from a current song or an old folk song, you can lead your class to the writing of a ballad on a topic you know will be of interest. Starting with the contemporary scene will work best. An examination of such songs will show that songs *do not* have to rhyme. From such study the teacher can then move students toward library research and the writing of historical ballads. Would any of these topics inspire an interest in ballad writing in your room?

Famous men and women
Athletic feats
Space adventures
Work songs
Explorers
Sea adventures
Sky adventures

Monsters
Science fiction
Tall tale heroes
Greek myths
American Indians

A sample ballad, written in the course of study about the westward movement, follows:

Westward Ho!

We forged ahead with spirit,
We stopped--but only to rest,
We trudged over hill and vale,
To meet our dream out West.

Refrain: Westward ho! Westward ho!
To the land we long to know!

Hunger was our companion,
Thirst and disease had their day,
But our mission was clear before us,
As we pushed on the western way.

Refrain: Westward ho! Westward ho!
To the land we long to know!

J. Romatowski

BALLADS
Spotlight a Person -- With a Ballad!

Ballads are songs which tell interesting stories about people, animals or events. Ballads may be recited as poetry or set to music and sung. They must contain a good rhythm (beat) but do not have to rhyme.

1.   Think of a person (real or fictional) on whose life you would like to concentrate. Write the name below.

_____
(Name)

2.   Use your library or current materials (magazines, newspapers, TV shows, movies) to gather information about your person. Make notes of your study.

3.   Using your notes, write a short ballad about the person. Try to include those things which you find most unique about the person.

The Ballad of _____
(Name)

_____

_____

_____

_____

_____

_____

_____

_____

_____

_____

_____

_____

By: _____

4.   Proofread and edit your ballad. Cut it out, mount it and decorate. Now share it with your class by displaying it.

POP SONGS

★ Music in all its forms has a direct connection with man's cultural and historical roots. This relationship is strongly apparent in popular music, as it manifests today's culture. Some composers of popular music write thoughtfully and reflectively. With serious intent they hold a mirror up to society, and their work is produced with a message in mind. These lyrics are not accidental; they do speak to young people and for young people.

Our modern balladeers may rightfully be acknowledged as the poets of the day. We all know that listening to pop songs is a great recreational pastime for the young. Because the songs speak in terms related to their lives, it is possible for them to draw some conclusions and relationships which are strongly expressed. A close examination of the lyrics of these songs reveals not only the versatility of language but statements about contemporary social issues as well. Among these are:

materialistic values	love and commitment
human relationships	ecology
Inroads of technology	war and peace
loneliness and alienation	brotherhood

Any activity involved with the analysis of the lyrics of popular songs is a labor of love since the children listen to the radio and to records with slavish devotion.

Encourage the students to listen to and write down the lyrics of favorite songs or ones at the top of the charts. Emphasize a search for lyrics that will point up figures of speech and poetic qualities of expression which they feel or have worked with in their lessons in poetic forms.

As a corollary, suggest that the songs they select should make statements of importance to them which they can interpret. Have each student title a poster board with the name of his/her song and attach a segment or some lines. The student may then add a personal analysis of his/her modern "pop" poem. The activity would be enhanced by an oral presentation for discussion of poetic language, denotative and connotative language and -- any other implications he/she may perceive. The treat of listening to a recording of the song under discussion would be a topper to the activity!

STUDENT WORK SHEET

POP SONGS

We all listen to popular songs either on the radio, on television, or on record players at home. The words or lyrics of these songs are modern poetry of a very special kind. They may be rhymed or unrhymed, serious or amusing, but they often say something to the listener. Interesting and unusual language is used in pop songs, just as it is in all forms of poetry. Here is an activity that will help you take a close look at some of your favorites.

Copy down all or part of the lyrics of a song you enjoy.

1. What is the title of the song? _____
    _____

2. In your own words, tell what the song is about. _____
    _____

3. Write down some poetic sounding language in the song. Use phrases or sentences.
    _____
    _____
    _____

4. List some colorful or strong words in the song (verbs, nouns and adjectives).
    _____
    _____
    _____

5. Find some combinations of rhyming words.
    _____
    _____

6. Can you think of some other titles for your song?
    _____
    _____

18

LIMERICKS

★ The limerick is a form of light verse, usually composed of five lines arranged in the following rhyming pattern:

Line 1 . . . . a
Line 2 . . . . a
Line 3 . . . . b
Line 4 . . . . b
Line 5 . . . . a

As you can see, lines 1, 2, and 5 rhyme and are usually longer than lines 3 and 4 which also rhyme.

The exact origin of limericks has not been established definitely. Edward Lear is credited with popularizing the limerick in the early years of the 19th century. Limericks are humorous, witty, ironic, and sometimes nonsensical. They are often used to ridicule politics, religion, convention, human mannerisms, or people of importance. At other times, they are simply funny and quite benign.

Here are some classic examples by Lear.

> There was an Old Man with a beard,
> Who said, "It is just as I feared! -
> Two owls and a hen,
> Four larks and a wren,
> Have all built their nests in my beard."

Bordering on the tongue twister, is this limerick by Lear.

A flea and a fly in a flue
Didn't know quite what to do
Said the flea, "Let us fly."
Said the fly, "Let us flee."
So they flew through a flaw in the flue.

It can be great fun to have your class select limericks to memorize and to act out. Such presentations are fun and provide a good laugh in a regular, busy school day. Your students can conduct their own library searches for limericks or you can have your librarian compile a collection of books which can provide the basis for a delightful learning center on limericks right in your room.

In the kind of learning center we're recommending, students should have all the necessary materials for:

1) making a poster of a favorite limerick and illustrating it

2) making and binding a small booklet of favorite limericks

3) writing limericks to various limerick starters prepared by the teacher.

After your students have enjoyed listening to and reading limericks, you will want to do some whole class writing of limericks. Be prepared with three or four starting lines. Remind your students of the rhyming pattern (have it on the chalkboard for easy reference).

Now, brainstorm with your class for other limerick lines. Be an active participant yourself. More often than not, you will find that the third line gives students trouble. Anticipate this and have some suggestions ready.

You have, no doubt, noticed that certain magazines and journals conduct limerick contests. Though we do not normally encourage competitiveness, students do enjoy "market-testing" their limericks for humor.

You may want to arrange a limerick writing contest in your class or between classes in your school.

LIMERICKS

Use Your "Funny Bone" -- Write a Limerick!

1. You have probably heard the poem printed below.

    There was a young lady of Niger,
    Who smiled as she rode on a tiger;
    They came back from the ride,
    With the lady inside,
    And the smile on the face of the tiger.
                                    anonymous

    This poem is a limerick. It is meant to be funny. Did you notice the rhyming pattern? Lines 1, 2, and 5 rhyme. Lines 3 and 4 rhyme also. These two lines are also a little shorter than the other three.

2. Try your hand at completing these limericks.

    There was once an athlete named Sam,

    _____

    _____

    _____

    _____

    A singer stepped up to the stand,

    _____

    _____

    _____

    _____

3. Copy a limerick which you think is especially good from a book!

    _____

    _____

    _____

    _____

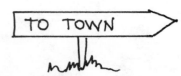
TO TOWN

PARODIES

★ A parody is the imitation of a particular style of someone else's work. A parody can treat a topic seriously or in a funny or ridiculous manner. If your students want to try the writing of parodies, remind them to acknowledge the original poet.

We are all familiar with the verses and the pleasant rhythm of Mother Goose rhymes. These rhymes and the poems of other poets can be used in interesting ways with your class.

A classroom activity that provides a fun experience with parodies is one where a familiar Mother Goose rhyme is used with the last line deleted. This "end-less" rhyme is placed on the chalkboard or recited by the teacher. The class supplies as many possible endings as they can. The only conditions to maintain are: 1) the ending must make sense with the preceding lines, and 2) the ending line must not be an offensive one in terms of language, in terms of particular people, or in terms of race, religion or someone's national origin. It would be sad, indeed, if in the process of a creative endeavor, the humanity of *any* student were diminished in any way. Mother Goose rhymes do lend themselves to silly, funny endings. The caveat issued is, therefore, quite important. Here are some silly endings to selected Mother Goose rhymes.

Jack and Jill
Went up the hill
To fetch a pail of water;
Jack fell down and broke his crown
And went straight to the hospital.

Humpty Dumpty sat on a wall
Humpty Dumpty had a great fall
And all the king's horses
And all the king's men
Enjoyed scrambled eggs for breakfast.

Old Mother Hubbard
Went to the cupboard
To get her poor dog a bone.
But when she got there
The cupboard was bare
Because things were bad all over.

USE A MODEL -- WRITE A PARODY

Writing a parody means using another poet's work as a writing model for a poem of your own.

1. Here is a Mother Goose rhyme you know.

    Hickory, dickory, dock!
    The mouse ran up the clock;
    The clock struck one,
    And down he run,
    Hickory, dickory, dock!

    Mother Goose

2. Use the starter below and create a different "Hickory, dickory, dock" poem. Use the same ending line.

    Hickory, dickory, dock!

    I see a hole in my sock;

    _____

    _____

    _____

    By: _____
    With acknowledgment to Mother Goose

3. Here is a poem by Lewis Carroll. It is from the story *Alice in Wonderland.* Read it and enjoy it.

    "The time has come," the Walrus said,
    "To talk of many things;
    Of shoes -- and ships -- and sealing wax --
    Of cabbages -- and kings --
    And why the sea is boiling hot --
    And whether pigs have wings."

    Lewis Carroll

4. Now, try writing a similar poem using the starter sentence given.

    "The time has come," the cowboy said,

    _____

    _____

    _____

    _____

    _____

    By: _____
    With acknowledgment to Lewis Carroll

NONSENSE POETRY

★ You will recognize this opening and closing stanza from Lewis Carroll's "Jabberwocky."

> 'Twas brillig, and the slithy toves
> Did gyre and gimble in the wabe:
> All mimsy were the borogoves,
> And the mome raths outgrabe.

This is a classic example of nonsense poetry. What does the poem mean? Your guess is as good as ours. Most of us would agree -- if not on meaning -- at least on the great fun it is to be able to recite this poem. Your students will enjoy it for the same reason.

You may be wondering why this poem seems to "roll off our tongues" so easily or why it is that we do not experience more trouble with intonation. We seem to know how to work the rhythm, where to pause, what to stress. None of us would read it as we would a shopping list. Intuitively, or very consciously, we know that the quality of the words selected by Carroll as well as their placement (in terms of word order) provide us with the clues we need to make good judgments about whether the word is a noun, an adjective, a verb, etc. Making this judgment, allows us to intone the poem properly. Writing nonsense poetry with your students (upper graders) will help them to internalize features of the English language, without your being pedantic about it. Such experiences -- as nonsense poetry --help them to understand how their own language functions.

The following strategy is recommended:

1. To prepare for the writing of nonsense poetry, some preliminary experience with nonsense prose is in order. Prepare a number of incomplete sentences with key words missing, for example,

a. You're the greatest _____ in the whole _____ _____.

b. In the land of _____, there _____ a _____.

c. We saw a _____ _____ who _____ in a _____.

At first, you may try completing the sentences by filling the slots with words which give the statement meaning. Then, brainstorm for all the nonsense words which could be used in place of the real words. Be careful to preserve the quality of the part of speech being replaced.

2. Read nonsense poetry to the class. Enjoy it. If you have difficulty finding nonsense poems, take any poem and change rhyming words or other key words to nonsense words.

3. Now, using couplets which will rhyme, prepare several first lines and have your class brainstorm for second lines where at least the rhyming word is a nonsense word. Here are some sample first lines. In parentheses a possible second line has been provided.

A) Why not live sweetly among the trees
   (clibbing and scarfing the youngarees)?

B) I wept with joy to hear your call
   (At ziddle to three at Nordoff stall).

C) Potato chips -- so light so thin
   (Are fried with Proxy-di-o-zin)!

D) The scarecrow struggles to keep his rags
   (But the wind blows them free like a jamofrazz).

4. You may want to have many more first lines prepared on slips of paper in a box. Have each student pick one and write a rhyming second line. Share orally and enjoy. Now have students exchange their slips of paper with neighbors. Repeat the process. Do this several times until everyone has three or four couplets.

5. Distribute fresh paper and have students select their favorite couplets, and write them in their best handwriting on the new paper.

6. Collect and display on a bulletin board or in the hallway of the school. An attractive copy of Carroll's "Jabberwocky" can provide the central focus for such a display.

NONSENSE POETRY

You really know more about your language than you think you do! You can make up all kinds of nonsense words for paragraphs or poems only to discover that there is a special quality to those words. That special quality marks that word as a noun, a verb, an adjective, etc.

Nonsense words have all kinds of possibilities. They are especially handy when you are looking for rhyming words for a fun poem.

1. Nonsense phrases

Complete these statements by filling in with a nonsense word. BE CAREFUL! Be sure that your nonsense word still makes your sentence sound like an English language sentence. Don't try to rhyme these.

We saw the _____ eat the _____.

The day was _____ and _____.

Can you _____ and _____ the _____?

2. Now try your hand at completing these couplets (two-line *rhyming* poems) with nonsense words.

Here I lie upon the sand,

_____

The drifting snow, and sleet, and ice,

_____

Over the net comes the serve,

_____

The hands of time pause not at all,

_____

3. Now! Compose your own nonsense sentences or nonsense couplets.

_____

_____

_____

_____

DEFINITION POETRY (SINGLE CONCEPT POETRY)

★ Definition poetry is a form of free verse which uses a selection of succinct phrases to define an idea or a concept. These are arranged in a particular pattern which appears in a later example.

Sometimes it is fun to take an idea, a concept, or even an object and brainstorm for all the images and emotive language this one theme evokes in the minds of all students. It is important to encourage picturesque, sensitive phrases which are brief and have a good balance of images and expressions of feeling. In teacher workshops, this technique can be used with the word "teacher" as the concept to explore. After filling the chalkboard with ideas from the group, write,

<u>What's</u> a teacher?

on the board. Now, ask the group to select a phrase from the board which would make an interesting second line. When selected, write it as the second line, but indent it five spaces. Then seven or eight more lines are selected and each is written on a separate line keeping the margin established by the second line. The group is then asked to think about tone and rhythm after the selection of each line. When finished, the ending line, "That's a teacher," can be written keeping the same margin as the *first* line. The completed definition poem looks like the following:

Teacher

What's a teacher?

> a friend and companion
>
> a sharer of knowledge
>
> dependable and caring
>
> fun to be with
>
> judge and arbiter
>
> referee and coach
>
> a planner, a designer
>
> a warm, sympathetic listener
>
> a human being worth knowing

That's a teacher!

Single concept poetry is fun to do with the entire class. There is an opportunity for vocabulary development and concept clarification with this free verse poetry. A fascinating discussion can evolve in the process of developing such a poem.

Here are topics that generate much discussion and call to mind many images and expressions of feeling. Perhaps some will be just right for your class.

fear	grandparents	night
grown-ups	a storm	love
war	a desert	racing
friendship	Hawaii	hockey
brother/sister	an argument	a friend
school	spring	courage
happiness	loneliness	a factory

Here is some free verse, definition poetry, written by a small group of fourth graders on the topic, courage.

Courage

What's courage?

reciting in class

wearing something different to school

taking your report card home

telling on someone who did something bad

backing down from a fight

passing the gang on the corner

arguing with your parents

That's courage!

DEFINITION POETRY

An easy way to write free verse is to pick a topic and define it by using short, colorful phrases. Such poetry is called definition poetry or single concept poetry.

1. Here are some ideas you may want to explore in writing your own definition poetry. Pick a topic or write in your own selection on the blank line.

a monster	fear	baseball
a nightmare	loneliness	swimming
a cemetery	friendship	snowmobiling
an amusement park	peace	

_____
(your choice)

2. Now think of at least twelve, short, poetic phrases and expressions for your topic.

_____   _____

_____   _____

_____   _____

_____   _____

_____   _____

_____   _____

3. Read your expressions carefully. Change them, if you need to, so that they are clear, strong expressions. Now select six of the best and complete this definition poem.

_____
(Title)

What's _____?

_____

_____

_____

_____

_____

That's _____!

By: _____

83

CLASSIFIED POETRY

★ Newspapers, magazines, and catalogs are a veritable storehouse of possible activities for the classroom. You have, no doubt, seen these materials used in the teaching of math, science, social studies, and all the language arts skills. A strategy for using these materials -- especially the advertisements -- for the writing of poetry might be called classified poetry.

As a group experience, this activity is especially effective. Distribute magazines to everyone in class. Have each student find as many advertisements as possible on one particular topic, for example, cars, tools, blue jeans, vacations, etc. Allow students to tear out all such ads and spread the collection before them. Collect the magazines so that they are not a source of distraction. Have your students read the ads carefully in search of good, short phrases or words which appear to be key words. Have a brainstorming session. List all contributions on the board. If the topic were cars, a partial list may look like this:

revered performance
comfort and convenience
personal luxury
the ultimate mark of quality
something quite uncommon
diesel-powered
built for you
leaner, trimmer
a blessing instead of a curse
a rare combination

enchanted by the styling
as good as it looks
exciting blend of handling and luxury
handcrafted detail
improved traction
clean, tight turning
open air pleasure
smoother ride
superior stability
an exhilarating car to drive

Now, with your whole class, decide on a good starting line. Select each line carefully -- pay attention to tone, rhythm and meaning. Title your poem or use the topic as the title. Possible poems may be:

My Car

Something quite uncommon
Superior stability
Clean, tight turning
Smoother ride
Handcrafted detail
A rare combination
As good as it looks
The ultimate mark of quality
A blessing instead of a curse.

Blue Jeans

Season to season
Blue jeans
Soft tailored
To fit your form
With the greatest of ease
Sensible because
The look is updated
A special collection.

CLASSIFIED POETRY

You can write a classified poem by using the clever, catchy phrases found in advertisements appearing in newspapers, magazines and catalogs. When you arrange these phrases in a pleasing order, you are writing the free verse called classified poetry.

1. Find an appealing topic -- something that is well advertised in newspapers and magazines. Here are some suggestions.

motorcycles	food	clothing
vacations	restaurants	perfume

2. Write your topic here. _____
You may want to use it for your title later.

3. Find as many advertisements as you can on your topic. Read them carefully. List all colorful, strong phrases and words found in the advertisements which describe your topic best.

_____	_____
_____	_____
_____	_____
_____	_____
_____	_____

4. Now select and arrange those phrases and/or words which together will make your poem. Be careful to make good sense and to keep good rhythm. Feel free to change or substitute words for a stronger effect.

_____
(Title)

_____

_____

_____

_____

_____

_____

_____

_____

_____

By: _____

CENTO - PATCHWORK POETRY

★ Patchwork poetry (cento) is a challenging activity for those students who not only enjoy reading and writing poetry but who also enjoy "playing around" with language. Patchwork poetry is aptly named inasmuch as it consists of creating a poem by selecting each line from a *different*, already existing, poem. Cento has a rhyme scheme --aa, bb, cc. The challenge comes in finding lines which work well together -- they *may* or *may not* rhyme. However, they must make sense when read as a total poem. Patience and a love of the search are necessary for this task. It does not make a good experience for small group (2-4) collaboration. Armed with a healthy supply of poetry books and perhaps a starter line from the teacher, the group can set out to meet the challenge.

A sample rhyming cento follows:

I saw a ship a-sailing,	a	(Mother Goose)
Blue sky prevailing.	a	(William Wordsworth)
Sweet day, so cool, so calm, so bright	b	(George Herbert)
Welcome all wonders in one sight.	b	(Richard Crashaw)
On this green bank, by thee, soft stream,	c	(Ralph Waldo Emerson)
Was it a vision -- or a waking dream?	c	(John Keats)

Involved in a search for patchwork poetry, students will need to employ a variety of language skills. They will need to attend to meaning; they will be making decisions regarding syntax (Is everything in the same person? Is the tense consistent?); they will be analyzing the rhyming elements in words. Further, they will be reading through large amounts of poetry and refining general reading skills.

As mentioned earlier, patchwork poetry requires much patience. The end result, however, can be quite gratifying and well worth the effort.

CENTO -- PATCHWORK POETRY

Cento is sometimes called patchwork poetry. It is well named because of the way it is put together. To make a patchwork poem, each line must be selected from a different poem. When the lines are put together, they must make sense. If you wish, you may make your poem rhyme.

Part I

1. Find a good copy of Mother Goose Rhymes or other poetry books. Take time to enjoy the poems.

2. Find a line in one rhyme which you particularly like, and make that the first line of your patchwork poem.

3. Now select lines 2, 3, and 4 in the same way. BE CAREFUL! Your poem must make good *sense*. Choose your lines carefully.

A Patched-Up Mother Goose

_____

_____

_____

_____

Part II

1.Use poetry books of your choice. Take the time to read and enjoy the poetry.

2. Now, create a longer cento (a patchwork poem) using various lines from the poems you've read.

A Cento

_____

_____

_____

_____

_____

_____

_____

_____

Part II

HAVING FUN WITH LANGUAGE: SKILLS AND MUCH MORE

Pressed to accomplish

Our assigned duty

Everyone looks for words.

Try as I might, I

Refuse any inspiration,

You try it.

Steve Guerriero, 1980

PART II

Writing Descriptively

Being able to express oneself on paper with clarity and skill is a goal worthy of attention in the classroom. Among the myriad of skills necessary for poetry writing is the ability to write descriptively. Such writing requires exposure to many examples and much practice.

In this chapter, those literary devices which are useful in poetry writing and which are easily learned by elementary and middle school students will be explored.

GENERAL INSTRUCTIONS

METAPHOR

★ The word metaphor is used in two different ways. A metaphor may be the general term for *all* figurative language. There may be as many as 250 different figures of speech! A metaphor may also be a particular word, phrase, or sentence which suggests a similarity between two things. The comparison between the two objects is only suggested. (The words like, as, than, similar to, resembles, may *not* be used. When such words are used to strike a comparison, the result is a simile.)

The following things are not alike but they share one similarity which helps us make a colorful metaphor. For example:

METAPHORS 1. The cloud is a white marshmallow. (They are both white, puffy, and soft looking.)

2. The road snakes around the mountain. (They both bend and curve.)

3. Elevators turn my stomach into a roller coaster. (They both go up and down dramatically.)

SIMILE

★ The figure of speech called a simile does much the same thing but uses intermediary words, such as like, as, than, similar to, resembles, etc., to highlight the comparison being struck. Some similes follow:

SIMILES 1. Without you I'm like a wave without a shore.

2. The old man gripped me like a vise.

3. She is as happy as a lark.

4. His mouth resembled a large cavern.

5. The mayor is as slippery as an eel.

In order to lead your students toward the use of figures of speech, highlight and discuss metaphor and simile during the reading of stories and poems. Equally important will be the number of whole-class experiences you provide your students in creating metaphors and similes. Third, encourage your students to use metaphors and similes, as you talk with them about a piece of writing. Fourth, acknowledge the use of metaphors and similes by students during the oral sharing of their writing.

You may want to bring something to class which is likely to generate a number of similes, for example, a piece of velvet, rough sandpaper, etc. Pass it among the students. Discuss all the things to which the piece of velvet can be compared. Write on the chalkboard:

"Velvet, as soft as...."

Have the students brainstorm for as many similes as possible. Vote on the six most interesting. Take the piece of velvet (mounted) and make it the center of a mobile. Hang the six similes from the mobile.

A similar plan can be used for instruction in the use of metaphor. List your key word, for example, "sandpaper" on the chalkboard. Brainstorm for all the things that could be described using "sandpaper" for comparison. Some examples follow:

The singer's sandpaper voice irritated the audience.

Dad's sandpaper beard scratched my cheek.

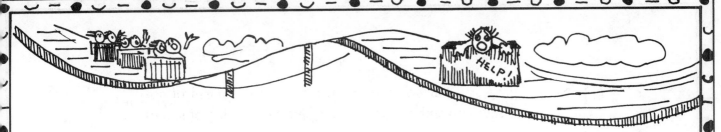

METAPHOR

The word metaphor is used in two different ways. A metaphor may be the general term for *all* figurative language. A metaphor may *also* be a particular word, phrase, or sentence which suggests a similarity between two things. The comparison between the two objects is only suggested.

The following things are not alike, but they share one similarity which helps to make a colorful metaphor. For example,

The *road snakes* around the mountain.   (They both bend and curve.)

Elevators turn my *stomach* into a *roller coaster*.

(They both go up and down dramatically.)

In the metaphors below explain how the two underlined things are similar. Why is one word used to describe the other?

1. Green *grass* is a *carpet* in the forest.

   _____

2. Her *eyes* were *diamonds* in the sunlight.

   _____

3. My *boss* is a *bear.*

   _____

4. The cowboy's *face* was made of tanned *leather.*

   _____

5. The *flowers* are summer's *crown.*

   _____

6. This is a *monster* of a *problem.*

   _____

7. That professional *wrestler* is a *gorilla.*

   _____

8. The *sentinel tree* stands guard at the gate.

   _____

9. Come here, old *gypsy dog*!

   _____

10. "*Juliet* is the *sun.*" (Shakespeare)

   _____

SIMILES

Writers often compare things to help the reader understand their messages. For example, if a writer wants you to really *see* -- in your mind's eye -- the blue of the sea being described in a poem or story, then comparing these two may help:

blue sea -- sapphires

Now, blue sea and sapphires are quite a bit different. But they share "blueness." The writer will use linking words, such as like, as, similar to, resembles, etc., in order to paint this picture in your mind. Such comparisons are called similes.

Example: The blue sea gleamed *like* a field of sapphires in the sun.

Try to write some similes yourself by completing the chart below. You will find this to be a handy tool as you write your own stories and poems.

NOUNS	ACTION WORDS	COMPARING WORDS	SIMILES
1. dog	ate	machine	The dog ate like a machine.
2. ear			
3. mosquito			
4. shark			
5. night			
6. gum			
7. storm			
8. snow			
9. hamburger			
10. sweater			

IMAGERY

★ When you describe a detailed picture of something in written or oral language, you have created an image in your listener's or reader's mind. The better able you are to create this image -- a mind picture or sensation -- the more effective is your communication. Thus, we say that the imagery in a piece of writing -- prose or poetry -- is either strong or weak. You will find, as you look for evidence of strong imagery, a dependence on words and phrases which have a strong appeal to the senses or to the emotions. You will also find dependence on figures of speech. To be strong, the imagery does not require particular length in terms of word count. Short statements can be as high in imagery as long statements. For example:

1. The highway was a swamp of cars.

2. The costumed dancers swarmed on stage in a brilliant riot of tropical colors!

It took a bit more to create the image desired in the second statement as opposed to the first. Indeed, in the first statement, the word "swamp" alone creates an image that is strong in terms of the message.

An interesting whole-class experience with imagery is to begin with a kernel statement and expand it in successive steps until a vivid image is created. Perhaps you could begin with this:

The car sped.

Ask your students to expand the statement by one word -- one which could be placed between "The" and "car." Are there ways to describe how fast the car sped (figure of speech)? Are there ways to expand the image by describing the site of the speeding car with a prepositional phrase -- (on the expressway)?

When you are finished with your expansions, you may have a series like this on your board:

The car sped.

The yellow car sped.

The flashy yellow car sped.

The flashy yellow car streaked.

The flashy yellow car streaked like a speeding bullet.

The flashy yellow car streaked like a speeding bullet along the wet freeway.

An important note here is to hold on to the original statement's message. Your goal is to make the initial statement come alive with imagery.

Another technique which works well is related to the above strategy and works best after a number of whole-class experiences. The strategy consists of giving each small group of students (3-4) the same kernel statement on which to expand. Have them follow the same procedures as were observed with the whole class in expanding the statement. Now, encourage them to use a thesaurus (make sure each small group has one or two) to look up their key describing words. Allow each group to read their final statements to the class. Pause to underscore the appeal to the senses, the use of emotive language and the effective use of figures of speech. A poster can be made featuring the kernel statement at the top and all the colorful statements below it. Or, such statements can be written on various colored 3 x 5 cards and used for a bulletin board display where the central balancing card contains the kernel statement only.

You may want to try the following activity with your class. Divide into small groups. Have each group select a *key* noun from a box. These *key* nouns will be used by the students as stimuli for the construction of phrases high in imagery. The *key* noun itself *will not* be used or revealed in the phrases the students develop. The nouns in the box will have to be carefully selected by the teacher prior to the activity. Nouns which instantly conjure up images in one's mind are:

KEY NOUNS

athletes	Halloween	elephant	jewelry
clouds	parades	trains	merry-go-round
flowers	orchestra	planes	snow
trees	puppy	statues	house

Now, have each small group make a list of images related to the key noun. Be sure that students understand that the use of strong imagery is central to the task. The key noun itself *must not* be used.* When lists have been compiled, have each small group read their entire list of images to the class without interruption. Then, have the class guess what the key noun was. Also, have the class relate to the group which were the strongest images in the list, which had a strong sensory appeal, which strongest emotional appeal, etc. The reinforcement here must stay positive. We want students to affirm each other's competence with language.

The use of imagery in writing is a worthwhile goal at any level. As the skill is nurtured by teachers, it begins to appear with increasing frequency in the oral language of students as well as in their written work -- both prose and poetry.

*Key noun: Stars

          Sky jewelry
          Night diamonds
          Precious evening glitter
          Incandescent sky lights
          Nature's heavenly neon
          Lustrous celestial canopy.

MAKE IT VIVID! USE IMAGERY!

When you speak or write in such a way that another person can clearly "see" what you are trying to communicate, then you are using good imagery. That means you are using words that appeal to the senses or to the emotions -- words that paint a clear picture in the reader's mind. It's the difference between saying:

> The roller skates were new and perfect.

and saying, instead:

> The new roller skates were made of gleaming stainless steel with speed built into every perfect wheel.

Below, you will find five ordinary statements. Using imagery, you can make them more vivid! More alive!

1. The volcano erupted.

_____

_____

2. The storm threatened.

_____

_____

3. The baby gorilla played.

_____

_____

4. The athlete ran.

_____

_____

5. The train moved on the track.

_____

_____

GENERAL INSTRUCTIONS

ONOMATOPOEIA -- THROUGH THE SOUNDS OF LANGUAGE

★ If you have ever selected a particular word in your writing because its sound reflected its meaning, you were most likely employing onomatopoeia. In today's world of print and even on TV, we are bombarded with instances of onomatopoeia: ZOOM, SWOOSH, ZAP, BOOM, etc. The use of onomatopoeia in writing provides a reader with a rich visual and auditory experience and helps to underscore the message of the writer. From the standpoint of effective communication then, helping to make your students aware of this device and teaching them how to use it should reap dividends in later writing.

It should be noted here that onomatopoeic language is not universal. In English we may characterize the dog's bark as "bow-wow" or "arf-arf." In another culture it may be "how-how." It would be a rich experience in language appreciation to examine these variations. Those students in your class whose home language is other than English or who have parents with close ties to their ethnic heritage would be excellent resources for such study. It would be important in such a study to help build pride in each ethnic group's use of language, to marvel at the human capability in creating language.

Along with such discussion, it would be interesting to display books written in languages other than English. This, too, would be a good experience in language appreciation. Think of the interesting charts that could be made displaying the variety of ways in which we characterize a dog's bark, a hen's clucking, or a human laugh through onomatopoeia.

A good, whole-class experience is to have your students identify onomatopoeic words to characterize words or phrases you place on the chalkboard. See how many such words your class can generate for the following words and phrases:

a human laugh	a coyote in the night
motorbikes	walking on peanut shells
a bell	a baby bird
water dripping:	brakes stopping
little drops	cracking of a whip
big drops	creaking of a door
a rooster	European police cars
car horns	eating potato chips

Such work can be transferred to a large poster and made accessible to your students in the writing corner. An added advantage of such study is the inevitable discussion about the spellings of various sounds and the incidental learning which occurs in such a setting.

Comic strips are a very rich source of onomatopoeia. Encourage your students to bring in the comics from the daily newspaper or their favorite comic books. Have your students browse through them and compile their own lists of onomatopoeic words. The chart could follow this framework:

	ONOMATOPOEIA	WHAT IT DESCRIBES
1.	Hee-haw hee-haw	a donkey braying
2.	Varoom! Varoom!	a sports car starting up
3.	Crash! Bam!	the ceiling falling down

LET'S HEAR IT FOR ONOMATOPOEIA!

Onomatopoeia is a term writers use for those words that sound like what they mean. No one would make a mistake in identifying which animal is represented by "oink oink" or what message is represented by "BOOM!" Being able to use onomatopoeia will help your writing come alive. Which of the following sentences create a better picture in your mind?

There was a large tuba in the parade.

"Umpa-pa, umpa-pa," went the large tuba in the parade.

He *ate* his soup.

He *slurped* his soup.

Try rewriting the sentences below using onomatopoeia. Make them sound alive.

1. The glass test tube exploded!

   _____

2. We walked in the mud.

   _____

3. I heard the drums of the marching band.

   _____

4. The car came to a sudden stop.

   _____

5. There was a terrible interference on the radio!

   _____

6. The motorcycle sped off.

   _____

7. The proud chicken announced that her egg had hatched.

   _____

8. His cane made sounds on the sidewalk.

   _____

9. The water went down the bathtub drain.

   _____

10. My skates went over the cement cracks.

    _____

PERSONIFICATION -- MAKING "IT" COME ALIVE

★ When a writer attributes human characteristics to those things which are clearly not human, this technique is called personification. The root word is a clue to how it came by this label. Perhaps in your own readings you have come upon passages from the sublime to the silly which employ personification.

"Tell wisdom she entangles herself in over-wiseness."

(John Lyly)

"With how sad steps, O Moon, thou climb'st the skies."

(Sir Philip Sidney)

"Love's not Time's fool, though rosy lips and cheeks
Within his bending sickle's compass come."

(Wm. Shakespeare)

".... and the dish ran away with the spoon!"

(Mother Goose)

For an easy whole-class activity, you may want to place on the chalkboard or on a transparency the following statements. Replace the underlined words or phrases with human actions:

The wind *blew* in the night. (moaned)
The outboard motor *made a noise*. (cleared its throat)
The leaves *fluttered* in the breeze. (danced)
The dog *sat upright* for his dinner. (scolded, begged, nagged)

It should be clear to your students as they replace the underlined sections with words usually ascribed to human behavior that the statement has changed qualitatively. The basic message has been conveyed, but in a more interesting way. And though you would not apply personification to everything you write, it does add variety and punch to writing where appropriate.

PERSONIFICATION -- MAKING "IT" COME ALIVE!

When you write about objects, things, ideas, and animals as if they were human, you are using personification. Do you see the root word "person" in the word *personification*? You will agree that this technique is well named. Look at how much more interesting it is to read!

Instead of: The cabin was at the side of the mountain.

Personify the cabin and write: The cabin clung for dear life to the side of the mountain.

Read the statements and questions. When you answer the questions, use personification in your answers and make these things come alive! Use complete sentences.

1.   The happy family moved out of the house. What did the house feel?

_____

2.   His breakfast oatmeal was in a bowl. How did the oatmeal feel or look?

_____

3.   The diseased tree was cut down. What did the tree think or feel?

_____

4.   The musician started to play on the tight new drums. How did the drums feel?

_____

5.   He popped the beautiful red bubble gum ball into his mouth. What did the bubble gum feel?

_____

6.   The robot was left behind by its master. How did it feel?

_____

7.   The strings on the guitar broke one by one. How did the guitar feel?

_____

8.   The boy took off his shoes and his toes poked out through the holes in his socks. How did his toes feel?

_____

9.   Broken and tossed aside, the toys were piled in a box. How did the toys feel?

_____

10.   The volume on the record player was turned high. What was the record player feeling?

_____

HYPERBOLE -- LET'S EXAGGERATE!

★ Hyperbole is a writing device which uses exaggeration to make a point. It can be used in prose and poetry and is heard in everyday oral language exchanges. Have you heard any of the following?

1. The hurdler jumped so high she touched the sky.
2. My father loves the whole world.
3. Make a sundae for me that's a mile high!
4. Coach Homer exploded with anger.
5. The stale cookie is as hard as a rock.

The study of hyperbole comes rather naturally when you are involved with your students in a study of tall tales. It would be very appropriate to introduce the writing of hyperbole at this time -- especially to display the aesthetic side of this device. For it is indeed true that many of our great and not-so-great authors and poets employ hyperbole in creative and imaginative ways to delight the reader. Here are some samples from the past.

Till a' the seas gang dry, my Dear,
And the rocks melt wi' the sun;
And I will luve thee still, my Dear,
While the sands o' life shall run.

(Robert Burns)

I asked my mother for fifteen cents
To see the Elephant jump the fence,
He jumped so high that he touched the sky
And never came back 'till the Fourth of July.

(Ray Wood
American Mother Goose)

Think of an interesting illustrated book that could be made to demonstrate our everyday uses of hyperbole. A good way to launch such an activity is to become a good observer/listener and make note of such language usage by your students. When you have collected a half-dozen such expressions, present them to your class for discussion. How effective was the exaggeration? What was really being communicated? How else could the same thing have been said, without hyperbole? Such discussions will not only heighten awareness about the use of hyperbole in communication but will lead to its use in later writing attempts.

A "fun" way to deal with hyperbole is by posing a question which will allow for exaggerated answers. For example, on the day following a particularly hot afternoon, you may want to write this on the chalkboard:

> How hot was it yesterday?
> It was so hot...

Now, invite your students to answer by completing the starter statement. Record all their endings in one long list.

> How hot was it yesterday?
> It was so hot...
>> that ice cubes melted in the refrigerator.
>> that you could fry an egg on the driveway.
>> that a layer of skin melted off my body.
>> that water boiled in the pipes.
>> the buildings were perspiring.

STUDENT WORK SHEET

LET'S EXAGGERATE -- USE HYPERBOLE!

When you deliberately exaggerate in writing or speaking because you want to create a strong effect, you are using hyperbole. You have heard people using hyperbole and you have used it yourself. Do any of these sound familiar?

"I am so hungry I could eat a horse."
"Donald, I've told you a million times to sit down."

Can you think of others you have heard around school or home? Below, you will find eleven questions to which the answers could be written using hyperboles. Answer in complete statements.

1. How big was the pizza?

    _____

2. How powerful was the truck driver?

    _____

3. How bad was the movie?

    _____

4. How sick did the roller coaster make the kids?

    _____

5. How fast is the car?

    _____

6. How mad was his father?

    _____

7. How much can you eat?

    _____

8. How boring was the class?

    _____

9. How loud was the rock group?

    _____

10. How hard are you working?

    _____

11. How happy were you on the last day of school?

    _____

Have fun comparing your hyperbole with your classmates.

ALLITERATION - SOME SOUNDS SOUND SWELL

★ When similar beginning sounds are used in two or more words close together, we get the effect of alliteration. It is fun and pleasing to the ear. How many times as a young child were you caught up in little rhymes and jingles like these:

> Thomas A. Tattamus took two T's,
> To tie two tups to two tall trees,
> To frighten the terrible Thomas A. Tattamus!
> Tell me how many T's there are in THAT.
>
> > Mother Goose

> Shimmy Sham Sham
> The Showboat man
> Shifted his show with
> She-nan-igans.
> > G. Lipson

Or perhaps you enjoyed this game:

> My name is Anna, I live in Ann Arbor, and eat apples.
> My name is Ben, I live in Babylon and eat bananas.

In each instance, it was alliteration -- the repetition of beginning sounds in words close together -- which gave the language its special flavor.

The names of people are the perfect starters for teaching alliteration. As a whole-class experience you may want to begin with your own first name or a fictitious name. Place it on the chalkboard and through expansion have your students develop it as completely as possible with as many words as possible which begin with the first letter of the name. If your name is John, your alliterative series may begin to look like this:

John
Joyful John jumps.
Joyful John jumps jubilantly.
Joyful John jumps jubilantly in jeans.
Joyful John jumps jubilantly in jam-stained jeans.

Here is a good opportunity to teach incidental things about syntax, about punctuation, etc. Even though the ultimate statement is silly-sounding, it is important to hold on to the "reasonableness" that is in the statement. It is important to be quite descriptive about what to include. When a student suggests a phrase containing too many *non*-alliterative words, acknowledge the effort by saying,

"Is there a way to make *every* word in the phrase start with the same letter?"
For example:

Rugged Rachel runs a rough, rigorous race.
Pamela the pilot prefers powerful, precision planes.
Bold Ben bakes big bagels.

Once your students have had fun with alliteration, invite them to create their own alliterative statements, using their first or middle names as starters. Encourage the use of the dictionary for word searches. Also, encourage working in pairs. Students can be marvelous resources for one another.

ALLITERATION -- REWARDING WRITING WITH REPETITION

When you use words that have the same or similar beginning sounds together, you are using alliteration. It is a clever technique which adds interest to your writing. It can be used for fun or for serious things. Here are some examples.

Sassy sister Suzy sat on a sofa and sobbed.
Warm and wistful woodwinds played wonderfully.

See how well you can compose alliterative statements. Create one sentence for each letter of the alphabet. Vary your statements. Make some serious and others not serious. Your dictionary will be a big help.

A - Amy always answers abruptly.

B - Bill bowls beautifully.

C - _____

D - _____

E - _____

F - _____

G - _____

H - _____

I - _____

J - _____

K - _____

L - _____

M - _____

N - _____

O - _____

P - _____

Q - _____

R - _____

S - _____

T - _____

U - _____

V - _____

W - _____

X - _____

Y - _____

Z - _____

FLOSSIE'S FRESH FISH

TONGUE TWISTERS

★ Tongue twisters are rhythmic patterns of language which use clusters of sound so similar that when the reader tries to read the statement, the jingle, or the rhyme, the tongue almost becomes twisted. Because they are so tricky to recite, they often prove to be a lot of trouble and there is nothing more to do but laugh. Try these -- increasing the speed with each recitation.

Theodore made three free phone calls.

The skunk sat on a stump
The skunk thunk the stump stunk
But the stump thunk
The skunk stunk.

How much wood would a woodchuck chuck
If a woodchuck would chuck wood?

Peter Piper picked a peck of pickled peppers;
A peck of pickled peppers Peter Piper picked;
If Peter Piper picked a peck of pickled peppers;
Where's the peck of pickled peppers Peter Piper picked?

Rubber baby buggy bumpers.

The sixth Sheik's sixth sheep's sick!

You will notice that it is more than alliteration that makes these tongue twisters troublesome. In many instances, it is the minimal difference between the sounds of the words or their internal features which make them difficult to pronounce. Note the examples on the next page.

stunk - thunk
Piper - pepper
sheik's - sheep's
stump - stunk
three - free
pickled - picked

You will have fun exploring tongue twisters with your students. It will surprise your class to discover that many of the tongue twisters popular today were equally popular when their teachers were growing up. Have your students interview their parents, grandparents, neighbors and friends to collect tongue twisters. The final collection could be quite impressive despite the duplications that are bound to occur.

Perhaps your class would enjoy a tongue twister tournament. The goal in such a tournament would be to provide an experience for memory development, as well as clarity and speed in speech, by using tongue twisters. To be fair, only two or three twisters of about the same length would be used in a tournament. Students would select one to memorize and to practice. The criteria of *speed* and *clarity* would be used to assess performance. Winners would be appropriately acknowledged.

Those students who continue to show an interest in such language work can form a tongue-twister committee. The goals of such a committee would be, first, to continue their library search for tongue twisters that the entire class might enjoy; and secondly, to write tongue twisters of their own for the class. Such activity can lead to the production of a deck of twister index cards for fun and games.

TROUBLESOME TONGUE TWISTERS

Do you recognize the tongue twisters printed below? Try saying them--slowly. Now repeat them several times, saying them more quickly with each repetition. Be careful! Be sure the words you are saying still sound clear. The listener must understand you.

Tongue Twisters:

Sister Suzy sat on a thistle.
She sells seashells at the seashore.
Bad butter makes batter bitter.

Complete these sentence starters, using word combinations that tangle your tongue. Change them any way you like!

a) The thrifty sisters _____

b) The terrible trucker _____

c) Twinkle toes tripped _____

d) Chocolate crumbled cookies _____

e) Madman Manny _____

f) Little lazy Lizzie _____

g) Pesty Patsy _____

h) Pulpy purple paper _____

i) Shimmering sunshine _____

j) Gurgling gerbils _____

k) Gooey globs _____

Write a tongue twister of your own. Challenge your classmates with it.

_____

_____

_____

_____

_____

USE YOUR SENSES!

★ We mentioned earlier, in the section on imagery, that writing which appeals to the senses can help enhance communication. Some concentrated sessions on using such "sensory expression stretchers" will make your students aware of this writing device.

A useful set of categories to stimulate the production of sensory words appears below. Can your students develop their own lists for these categories?

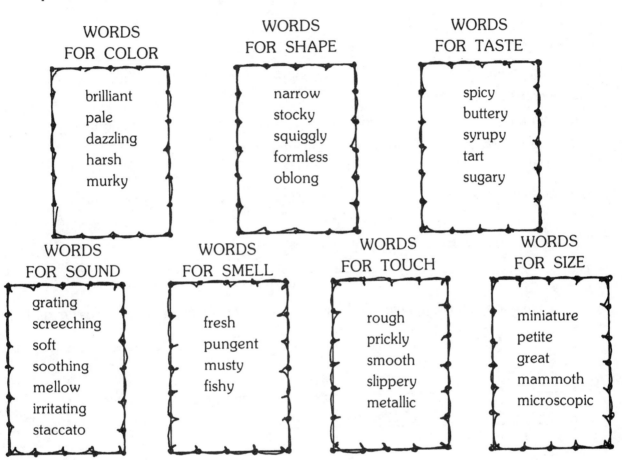

WORDS FOR COLOR
- brilliant
- pale
- dazzling
- harsh
- murky

WORDS FOR SHAPE
- narrow
- stocky
- squiggly
- formless
- oblong

WORDS FOR TASTE
- spicy
- buttery
- syrupy
- tart
- sugary

WORDS FOR SOUND
- grating
- screeching
- soft
- soothing
- mellow
- irritating
- staccato

WORDS FOR SMELL
- fresh
- pungent
- musty
- fishy

WORDS FOR TOUCH
- rough
- prickly
- smooth
- slippery
- metallic

WORDS FOR SIZE
- miniature
- petite
- great
- mammoth
- microscopic

These categories can serve as the basis for the construction of continuing sensory charts. Such charts can be placed in the writing corner and used as a resource by students for future writing.

For a more in-depth experience in sensory writing, you may want to focus your attention on a theme. Let us suppose that you listed "Memorial Day" as your stimulus. Brainstorm with your class for sensory expressions associated with this holiday.

Memorial Day

SIGHT	SOUND	TASTE

SIGHT
marching bands
old veterans marching
flags waving
family get-togethers

SOUND
firecrackers popping
trumpets blaring
children crying
politicians yakking away

TASTE
barbecued hot dogs
salty popcorn
cool, refreshing beverages

SMELL
smoked-filled parks
fresh air
roasting marshmallows
sweaty crowds

TOUCH
hot, clammy skin
prickly grass
steaming rays of sun
cool lake breezes

When enough has been recorded, invite your class to create a free verse using this format:

Memorial Day

I see _____

I hear _____

I feel_____

I smell _____

I taste _____

I know _____

Be careful to keep the tone consistent. This is done by simply asking after *each* line, "What could we write here (next line) to keep the same spirit going?"

Here is a possible end product.

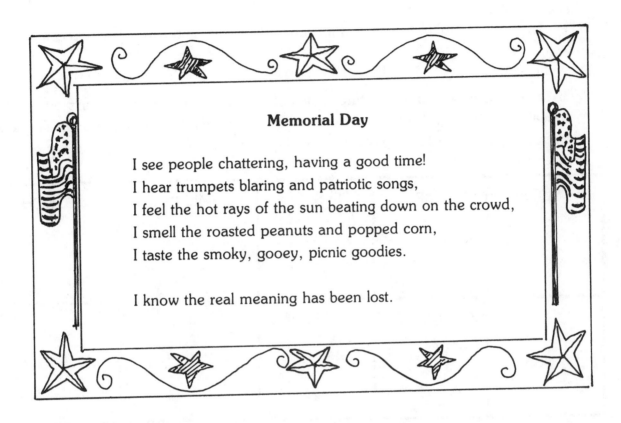

Memorial Day

I see people chattering, having a good time!
I hear trumpets blaring and patriotic songs,
I feel the hot rays of the sun beating down on the crowd,
I smell the roasted peanuts and popped corn,
I taste the smoky, gooey, picnic goodies.

I know the real meaning has been lost.

You noticed, no doubt, that the "I know" statement is meant to serve as a punch line, as a summary, as a reflection, as a philosophical statement. The time to discuss this statement is at the moment of writing it. It should not enter into the earlier discussions. However, all the prior discussion will help in its formation. This is the reason for setting it off from the rest of the poem.

All of the holidays and most festive events such as a circus, a fair, a carnival, a birthday party, etc., can help your students build their repertoire of sensory expressions.

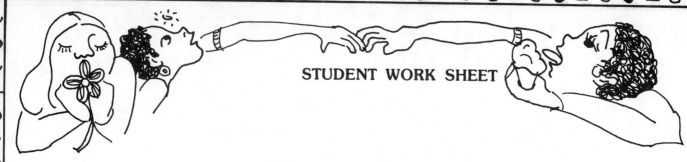

STUDENT WORK SHEET

USE YOUR SENSES!

1.   Select a colorful picture from a magazine. It should be one you feel you can describe well.

2.   Study each detail of the picture. Think of words to describe these details --words that appeal to the senses. Write your words below. Use only those categories which are appropriate for your picture.

SEE	HEAR	TASTE	SMELL	TOUCH
	CONTRIBUTIONS FROM THE THESAURUS			

3.   Look up your words in a thesaurus. Can you find stronger words which describe your picture even more clearly? Write them into your chart.

4.   Place an asterisk (*) after five words which you feel are the very best.

5.   Write a one-sentence description of your picture. Use words from the lists above. Keep revising until you are satisfied with your description.

_____

_____

_____

_____

GIVE A CHEER!

★ Cheers are constant reminders to us of how much people enjoy having fun with language. What athletic event or pep rally would be complete without cheers? The chorus of voices and the high feelings truly enliven the sport and create spirit.

If your school uses cheers, then you have a starting point for enjoying cheers as well as inspiration for writing them. Using your children as resources is always helpful. There may be some students who have brothers or sisters, neighbors or friends who are in high school or in college. They would have access to people who know some cheers. How about discussing cheers with parents, too?

Some interesting language learning can take place quite incidentally in such study. Spelling is an obvious area that comes to mind. Looking for rhyming elements in words is another. Understanding how we shorten words to accommodate rhythm is a third. Here is an example.

Put to the test,
We do the best!
Break 'em, Take 'em,
Ziss Boom Ba!

One way in which to foster some class spirit or school spirit is by writing cheers. Upper elementary and middle school students are particularly good at this. Again, it is important to note here that such writing must flow from experience. One must feel the enjoyment of a cheer and internalize its features before being asked to write one. The writing of cheers is particularly good group work. And of course you will want your students to perform the cheers they write. Cheers are written to be performed by a vigorous chorus.

School pep rallies and athletic events would be much less fun without a good, old cheer to stimulate school spirit. All school cheers have strong rhythmic qualities. Many also depend on strong rhyme. Here are two examples.

Cheerleaders
spell out
the first 7
lines.

Thirkell School

T-h

T-h

T-h-i-r

k-e

k-e

k-e-l-l

T-H-I-R-K-E-L-L

Thirkell!

Central High

My, My

Flying High

Live or Die

For Central High

RAH, RAH, RAH!

GIVE A C-H-E-E-R!

School pep rallies and athletic events would be much less fun without a good, old cheer to stimulate school spirit. All school cheers have a strong, definite beat. Many also depend on strong rhyme. Here are two examples.

Put to the test,

We do the best!

Break 'em, Take 'em,

Ziss Boom Ba!

We all really

Know the score

Block 'em,

Knock 'em

To the floor!

1. Choose a partner. Write a cheer you have heard. To be sure that others can read the cheer with the proper rhythm, pauses and expression, have your partner read it back to you.

_____

_____

_____

_____

_____

_____

2.   Try writing a cheer for your class, for your school, for your city or state. Teach it to your fellow classmates or organize a group of cheerleaders to perform it.

_____

_____

_____

_____

_____

_____

JINGLES

★ Even the casual TV viewer must be aware of jingles in advertising. These same, simple, rhythmic patterns of language can also be heard on radio and seen in print. Jingles make catchy advertisements which consumers can easily remember. Very often jingles are simple rhyming poems. At times they are set to music.

It would make an interesting listening/reading assignment to have your students record jingles they have seen or heard for a one-week period. An examination of such jingles in class can lead to a better understanding of how they are created. Further, they offer the teacher a good opportunity to explore propaganda techniques with students.

The writing of jingles is a good small-group activity. Distribute magazine pictures to each small group. Be certain that there are no identifying brand name labels on the items pictured. Have your small groups decide on a brand name for the item. Then, give them the necessary time to create a jingle and feature it on a poster along with their picture. These posters, when displayed in the school hallway, provide some fun reading experiences for everyone. Here is a sample. It could easily be put to music and performed in class.

> Old Grit Cleanser
> It's always fine,
> Chases dirt and saves you time!
> Look out grime!

Some ordinary items which lend themselves well to jingle writing are listed below.

cereal	sneakers	hamburgers
sunglasses	calculators	perfume
deodorant	candy	shampoo
blue jeans	motorbikes	pizza
soda pop	sports equipment	ice cream
bikes	vacation spots	gum

WRITING JINGLES

When companies want to sell a product or a service they advertise with a catchy jingle or a slogan so that people will really remember the product. Jingles are poems that have an obvious easy rhythm with a simple repetition of sounds. The catchy quality of a jingle often stays in our heads when we hear it over and over again. This is just what the advertiser wants. Jingles or slogans can be sung, chanted or recited. For example:

Product: Bubble gum

Jingle: Snap our gum
        It's a double bubble.
        No stress or stick
        To make you trouble.

Product: Tennis racquet

Jingle: Better grip,
        Stronger frame,
        Make your tennis
        A winning game!

1. Write your favorite commercial jingle here.

Product: _____ Brand name: _____

Jingle: _____

_____

_____

_____

2. Select items for which you would like to write a jingle. If you wish, you may invent a product, then write a jingle to advertise it.

Product: _____ Brand name: _____

Jingle: _____

_____

_____

_____

_____

Product: _____ Brand name: _____

Jingle: _____

_____

_____

_____

_____

_____

GREETING CARD MESSAGES

★ We are a card-sending society. No occasion eludes the card-making companies. For all we know, some occasions may have been established by them, for obvious reasons. Greeting card messages can be long or short, serious or funny, sentimental or businesslike. Your students may enjoy bringing in old cards from home for the class to listen to and discuss. They would make a colorful display. Do screen the cards that come in, very carefully. Greeting cards with offensive language or those which contain demeaning references to a person's racial, religious or ethnic background would not be appropriate for the classroom. Handling such a situation with a student would have to be done sensitively so that the student would understand the value involved. Think of all the occasions which present themselves during a school year for writing greeting card messages. Here is a sampling.

Birthday	Wedding	Graduation
Bar Mitzvah	Get Well	Christmas
Confirmation	Thank You	Hanukah
Anniversary	New Baby	Valentine's Day
Sweetest Day	New House	Easter
Father's Day	Thinking of You	St. Patrick's Day
Mother's Day	Bon Voyage	Halloween

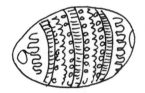

When the occasion presents itself, prepare to spend some time with your entire class writing a number of simple greeting card messages on the board. Be prepared with some possible first lines (your classroom collection of old cards could be tapped as a resource). Have your students work together as a class in completing the message. Here are some messages for different occasions from *It's A Special Day,* by Greta B. Lipson, Good Apple, Inc., ©1978.

My Valentine

Sometimes we wait
For a special day
To tell someone
In a special way,
That a friend means a lot,
If he's kind and true.
My valentine wishes
Say that to you!

Mother's Day

Today you don't need
sugar
I really want to say
My love will sweeten
everything
You touch on Mother's
Day.

Father's Day

My heart tells me true
The things about you
That make me very proud.
Your strength and your love
Help keep me above
The rest of the rag-tag
crowd.

Writing and making greeting cards is a good idea for a permanent learning center in your room. All paper materials, tools, decorative items, old card display, etc., could be located at the center. Students often find a need to create a greeting card for the family and friends. When students are moved toward such a thoughtful gesture, having all materials readily available in class will be very important.

GREETING CARD MESSAGES

On special days we like to send greeting cards to our friends and loved ones. There are companies that specialize in greeting cards for all occasions. Some of these cards are funny and some are serious. If you look at a rack of these cards in the store, you will notice that they are designed to include everybody--mothers, fathers, brothers, sisters, grandmothers, aunts, uncles, babies and many more. Inside the cards may be found rhymed messages that are simple but pleasant to receive.

Look through some of your old cards at home or at school for ideas. Write a message of your own that is funny and one that is serious. You may want to use starter lines or rhyming words from your card collection.

FUNNY MESSAGE

Occasion: _____

_____

_____

_____

_____

_____

_____

_____

SERIOUS MESSAGE

Occasion: _____

_____

_____

_____

_____

_____

_____

_____

FLAMBOYAN
SUPERCALARAGALISTICEY
QUANTATATIVN

GENERAL INSTRUCTIONS

COMPACT LANGUAGE -- DOING THE HINKY-PINKY!

★ Compact language, the hinky-pinky, terse verse, all relate to the same thing, for example, the use of two rhyming words to define something or answer a question. For example:

(definition type)
    A sneaky insect: Sly fly
    A carpenter: A hammer slammer
    A messy assignment: Sloppy copy

(question/answer type)
    What did the fish say to the bait? Squirm worm
    What did you call a villainous clergyman? A sinister minister

These can prove to be fun experiences with language. You will find that upper elementary and middle school students enjoy them considerably and love to create them. Starting with the rhyming words first is easiest. Then write the definition or the question to match your hinky-pinky. Incidentally, you and your students can be analyzing the rhyming elements in words, sharpening dictionary skills by using the dictionary to verify word choices, and examining the technique of writing appropriate questions and/or definitions. And, of course, there will be growth in vocabulary also.

Once you have had a sufficient amount of whole-class experience with compact language, you may want to challenge your class with the following activity. Have each student -- or a pair -- develop his own hinky-pinky with an appropriate question or definition statement. After each hinky-pinky has been discussed with you, then have it prepared on a small poster board. The question or definition statement should be carefully printed on the top half. The hinky-pinky should be written on the bottom half and then covered with a 5 X 7 card. The flap can be raised to reveal the hidden hinky-pinky. Collect all the posters. Number each one. Display them in order around the room or in your school hallway. Now, have each student number a sheet of paper with as many numbers as there are posters. Allow the students to browse through the posters (everyone does not have to start with number 1). Let them guess at the hinky-pinkies. When everyone has had sufficient time to write down the guesses, have the creator read the question or statement and reveal the hinky-pinky.

Student's Name: Alfred Blain

What do you call an archeologist who studies pyramids and mummies?

Answer behind flap

A Tut nut!

Think of the language fun and excitement which can be generated in the entire school if these are displayed in a hallway. Even parents walking through the building will find them delightful.

You and your students may enjoy writing questions or definitions for the following terse verses:

Jelly belly

Fat cat

Gooey chewy

Fast mast

Horse course

Cool fool

Billow pillow

Bug hug

Net pet

Top cop

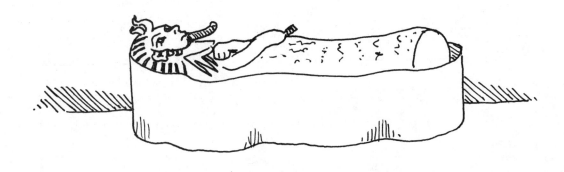

COMPACT LANGUAGE -- DOING THE HINKY-PINKY!

The word terse describes a statement that is compact, to the point, and free from extra words. This describes terse verse or hinky-pinky. A couple of words say it all! You can write terse verse in two ways: using the question/answer pattern or using the definition pattern. For example:

Question/Answer Pattern: What do you call a film on disco dancing? Groovy movie.

Definition Pattern: Boob Tube -- a television set.

Try writing your own hinky-pinky or terse verse. Write your rhyming words first. Then decide on your question or definition.

TERSE VERSE	QUESTIONS OR DEFINITIONS
1. _____	1. _____
2. _____	2. _____
3. _____	3. _____
4. _____	4. _____
5. _____	5. _____
6. _____	6. _____
7. _____	7. _____
8. _____	8. _____
9. _____	9. _____
10. _____	10. _____

CHARMS, SPELLS AND BLESSINGS

★ Since ancient times human beings have invoked the spirits in times of happiness and stress. People have tried to summon assistance from "on high" to get support and succor. Sometimes we call for help from darker worlds to punish those who have given us pain. Our charms, spells and blessings may be solemn or joyous, depending upon the situation.

The oral and written tradition of folklore is rich with these requests for help, inspiration and protection. Equally as popular is the beckoning of evil spirits expressed in witchcraft or exorcism. The most popular of these incantations was written by William Shakespeare in the witches' scene in *Macbeth*:

"Double, double toil and trouble;
Fire burn and cauldron bubble."

Sweeter by far are the blessings which ask for divine favor and are hopeful of happiness in the future. The following Irish blessing is a clear example of this:

May the road rise up to meet you
May the wind be always at your back
May the sun shine full upon your face
May the rain fall gently on your fields,
And may the good Lord keep you in the hollow of his hand
Until we meet again.

Here is another.

Blessings on thee, little man,
Barefoot boy, with cheek of tan.

                    John Greenleaf Whittier

Charms, spells and blessings may be regarded as word formulas which may or may not rhyme. But always there should be a lyric, rhythmic quality which appeals to the ear. Remember that charms are always positive but spells may be either good or bad!

Read some charms, spells and blessings to the students. Have them research in the library in folktales and fairy tales for more of the same. Encourage the students to ask at home for blessings and spells that pique the imagination. Record and discuss these contributions and then encourage the children to write their own. Many of the sayings may lend themselves well to creative illustrations. For example:

May you grow like an onion
With your head in the ground
And your feet in the air.

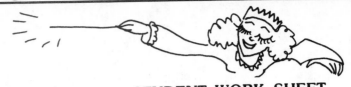

CHARMS, SPELLS AND BLESSINGS

Sometimes, we call upon little sayings or blessings to help us through the day. When we wish other people good luck and good health, we are doing the same thing for others. Do you remember that some characters in the old folktales would often cast charms or spells upon others? Charms and spells are sayings that will produce magical effects (if you believe in magic). Charms always produce good magical effects but spells produce *either* good or bad results. Here are some examples.

A Blessing:

    Watch over me from feet to ears,
    Protect me through the passing years.

                                G. Lipson

A Charm:

    All powerful Maker of Magic,
    Cast a spell over me --
    Change me in the eyes of each beholder,
    Make me the star athlete to my coach;
    Bright and smart to my teacher;
    A strong and true friend to my companions;
    The perfect child at home.
    Do all this, Maker of Magic --
    But don't really change the me I am!

                                G. Lipson

A Spell:

    May billows of rain clouds
    Visit the school athletic field
    And wash out the cheating team.

                                G. Lipson

Now that you understand the differences in blessings, charms and spells, try writing some of your own. Make them fit your situation.

Write a blessing. _____

_____

_____

_____

Cast a spell on an evil person or thing. _____

_____

_____

_____

Work up a charm to do a job. _____

_____

_____

EPITAPHS - ONE LAST LANGUAGE FLING

★ An epitaph is, most generally, a short statement in prose or poetry that is meant to memorialize someone who has died. Often it is carved into a tombstone. A walk through a cemetery will yield an interesting variety of epitaphs. Some may be quite serious or quite sweet; others may be funny or downright satirical. Epitaphs have a long history. You may have encountered the following examples in your study of literature:

My Own Epitaph

Life is a jest; and all things show it;
I thought so once, but now I know it.

John Gay
(17th Century)

Epitaph

Here lies my wife; here let her lie!
Now she's at rest--and so am I.

John Dryden

These two examples are brief two-liners and quite typical. However, epitaphs are not restricted by length. William Cowper's "Epitaph on a Hare" ran forty-four lines. Your students will find the writing of two-line and four-line epitaphs most manageable.

The reading of epitaphs to your class, library searches or a trip to a local cemetery to collect epitaphs is the most reasonable starting point. Once you have helped lead your students to an appreciation of epitaphs, then writing can begin. Such writing could be easily correlated with a unit on biographies. Writing epitaphs for famous people whose accomplishments are quite vivid is good for whole-class activity. Write the famous person's name on the board (the person does not need to be dead) and allow for a discussion of accomplishments. Brainstorm for possible first lines. Next, brainstorm for rhyming words to the ending word of the first line. Now, use the list to construct your second line. An epitaph follows:

An Epitaph for a Country Music Star

He played his fiddle with zest and joy
'Cause he loved bein' a country boy!

Comic epitaphs are fun to write. Sometimes these are easier to write when we do not have a specific person in mind. Try writing a light sounding or funny sounding epitaph for the following people:

movie star	Dracula
cowboy	opera singer
astronaut	teacher
ballet dancer	waiter
jockey	chef
bowler	hunter

Here are some examples.

Here he lies, good Doctor Platt,
A taste of his medicine knocked him flat.

G. Lipson

Here lies a singer
Who had a sweet throat,
Alas for us all
She's sung her last note.

G. Lipson

Here lies the village baker
He used to bake our pies.
He's happy now in heaven
And baking in the skies.

G. Lipson

Here lies Tillie
With a hole in her head;
A ball came and hit her
And now she's quite dead!

G. Lipson

FUNNY EPITAPHS

An epitaph is a short statement in prose or poetry that is inscribed on a gravestone in memory of the person who is buried there. These inscriptions are usually serious and sad, but sometimes they can be funny. With a humorous spirit write some of these epitaphs for comic figures. You may use the rhyme scheme of your choice but an easy pattern is the following:

For example: Here lies Kelly (a)
Oh he was quite the knave (b)
He's staying out of trouble now (c)
A resting in his grave. (b)

G. Lipson

He left his house (a)
To cross the street (b)
He didn't know (c)
A car he'd meet. (b)
Rest in peace.

G. Lipson

Try writing epitaphs of your own. You may select people from the list below or think up your own.

fisherman	policeman	pizza maker
football hero	carpenter	cook/chef
dancer	coach	nurse
rock star	tailor	golfer

Epitaph for _____

_____

_____

_____

Epitaph for _____

_____

_____

_____

Epitaph for _____

_____

_____

_____

For all intents and purposes
This document is real

It tells the world just what I am
And what I truly feel

I have the poet's right to write
Create and make with words

I'll fashion them with care and skill
My license to observe.

POETIC LICENSE _____

POETIC LICENSE IS AWARDED TO _____

IN ACCORDANCE WITH THE PROVISIONS OF LYRIC EXPRESSION.

ON THIS MONTH OF _____ IN THE YEAR OF _____

THIS LICENSE ENTITLES THE BEARER TO COMPOSE POETRY IN ALL

DIVERSE FORMS. ISSUED WITH DISTINCTION IN ROOM _____

SIGNED BY MY HAND _____
(Teacher)

SCHOOL _____

CITY _____

STATE _____

Poetic License

You can't buy it,
You can't sell it;
You just have it,
And once you have it
The language is yours.

_____
POETIC LICENSE

POETIC LICENSE IS AWARDED TO _____
IN ACCORDANCE WITH THE PROVISIONS OF LYRIC EXPRESSION.
ON THIS MONTH OF _____ IN THE YEAR OF
THIS LICENSE ENTITLES THE BEARER TO COMPOSE POETRY IN ALL
DIVERSE FORMS.   ISSUED WITH DISTINCTION IN ROOM _____

SIGNED BY MY HAND _____
(Teacher)

SCHOOL _____
CITY _____
STATE _____

I'm a poet with a license,
And it's right up front to see
That everyone can have it
Even you and me!

You take some thoughts and shape them
And find the words to say,
Some things about your feelings
In your own special way.

POETIC LICENSE _____

_____

POETIC LICENSE IS AWARDED TO _____

IN ACCORDANCE WITH THE PROVISIONS OF LYRIC EXPRESSION.

ON THIS MONTH OF _____ IN THE YEAR OF _____

THIS LICENSE ENTITLES THE BEARER TO COMPOSE POETRY IN ALL

DIVERSE FORMS. ISSUED WITH DISTINCTION IN ROOM _____

SIGNED BY MY HAND _____
                          (Teacher)

SCHOOL _____

CITY _____

STATE _____

INDEX OF POETIC FORMS AND FIGURES OF SPEECH